Of Moose and Miracles
A Mother's Story of Her Beloved Son

Written by
Marion Lee

As told by
Karyl Frick

OF MOOSE and MIRACLES
The Kraig Frick Story

ISBN#1-891280-42-2
Copyright © 2002 Marion Lee (Author)
2nd Printing, 2008

Publisher: CMJ Marian Publishers & Distributors
Post Office Box 661
Oak Lawn, Illinois 60454
Phone: 708-636-2995
www.cmjbooks.com
jwby@aol.com

Graphic Design: Lisa Duffy
Editorial Assistance: Cynthia Nicolosi

Manufactured in the United States of America

A Note of Gratitude

I thank all the angels and saints in heaven and all the people on earth who prayed and cared for Kraig.

I thank Father Jacques for binding our families and most especially for sharing his priestly ministry with Kraig.

My gracious thanks to Marion Lee for taking what is in my heart and putting it into words on paper, making this book possible.

I thank my family for all their love, care and understanding.

I thank Jesus and our Mother Mary for their constant compassion and love and for never once having to explain to them the pain I feel.

I thank You, God, for Kraig.

Karyl Frick
Dallas, Texas

Dedicated with love to the Frick family in heaven and on earth.

"For everything there is a season,

and a time for every matter under heaven…

He has made everything beautiful in its time."

(Eccles. 3:1,11)

TABLE OF CONTENTS

Acknowledgments

Acknowledgments

Writing this book became a labor of love for me; yet, had it not been for the tenacity of my friend, Mary Murphy, it would never have happened. Mary insisted that I contact a woman named Karyl from her prayer group to discuss the possibility of a story about her son. I was more than reluctant to contact a perfect stranger, but Mary's persistence wore me down. I finally made the initial call only to discover that Karyl was slated for surgery and could not commit to a meeting any time soon. Relieved, I put the matter out of my mind until the day an excited Mary approached me with Karyl in tow. Whatever fears I may have had evaporated at that first meeting. Karyl and I had an immediate rapport, and when she began to talk about Kraig, I knew this was a story that had to be shared. My only reservation was whether or not I would be capable of doing it justice.

Once a week, with tape recorder in hand, I sat at Karyl's kitchen table covering a wide array of stories about her wonderful family. I also had the privilege of interviewing others for this book, most notably Father Jacques LaPointe, OFM, a remarkable person whose warmth and charm immediately attract.

At Karyl and Mike's invitation, I traveled to Colorado and spent time at their cabin. Such a gorgeous setting proved to be an enormous help in moving forward with the story. While there, I had the pleasure of visiting St. Malo's Chapel, the site where the story begins.

I had never had the privilege of meeting Kraig Frick, yet I can say with all honesty that I have come to love this child who has lived in my heart and mind from the first day I sat down with his mother. Through Kraig, Karyl and I have become close friends. Karyl's faith, courage, and ability to recognize the joy of life even in the face of tragedy is edifying to all who know her.

As you experience God's loving touch in this story, may it bring your loved ones here and in the hereafter closer to you, and may the peace of God, which surpasses all understanding, be yours now and forever.

Marion Lee
Lancaster, Pennsylvania

About the Author

Marion Lee was born and educated in Pittsburgh, Pennsylvania. She laughingly says that her first brush with fame came at the tender age 10 with the publication of a poem in a popular children's magazine. "It was a *long* time between success stories!" In 1982, *Good Housekeeping Magazine* published a story about the miracle birth of her third child, and this proved to be the launching pad for all future stories. Marion's first book, *"On the Palm of His Hand,"* was published by St. Bede's in 1988. Since then, she has written several short stories that have appeared in a variety of magazines.

Marion and her husband, Edward Levandowski, just recently celebrated their 44th wedding anniversary. They are the parents of three grown daughters and the proud grandparents of four beautiful grandchildren. Both retired, Marion and her husband live in Lancaster, Pennsylvania.

Chapter I

For Everything, a Season (Eccles. 3:1)

I will never forget the day Jacques entered our lives, and when I reflect on all that has happened since then, it overwhelms me.

I was vacationing with my family in Colorado. It was Sunday morning, and I had volunteered to drop a few of the kids off in town to go water rafting. On the way back to our cabin, I decided to stop by St. Malo's Chapel, the beautiful church visited by the Holy Father in 1993 when he was in Denver for World Youth Day.

I know now that some kind of heavenly logic was at work that day. St. Malo's is no ordinary place. The Chapel on the Rock, as it is sometimes called, is surrounded by stately pines and a small brook that looks somewhat like a medieval moat protecting a castle. Across from the entrance stands a massive white marble statue of Christ with his right arm outstretched, pointing in the direction of the chapel. The gesture has special significance: one could say that St. Malo's exists today because heaven itself pointed out the spot. On an August night in 1916, a young priest and avid mountaineer named Joseph Bosetti saw a meteor fall into the area. He never found the remains of the celestial messenger, but he did discover an impressive rock formation which he believed would be the ideal place for a chapel.

The Malo family of Denver was one of the first benefactors and because there actually is a "St. Malo" from Brittany, France, St. Malo's seemed an appropriate choice to name the chapel. With the blessing of the bishop of Archdiocese of Denver, and the financial support of the Malo family, Mon-signor Bosetti oversaw the development of Camp St. Malo, which eventually evolved into the St. Malo's Retreat Conference Center. An attractive, three-story lodge situated high above the chapel was added in 1987. The spectacular setting of the center, which now serves as a hermitage for people of all faiths, cannot help but draw souls toward the creator of all things.

As I approached St. Malo's, I could see that the gate was unlocked and the wooden door leading into the chapel was slightly ajar. I also noticed that the parking lot was empty. I was delighted since this meant I could spend some quiet time alone in prayer. When I entered the chapel, however, I was taken aback by the sight of a group of men kneeling for a Mass that had already begun. I quietly slipped into a pew in the back and began to pray, half wondering who these people were and whether or not I should be there. Strangely enough, I felt very welcome.

An inspiring homily followed the Gospel. Toward the end, the priest looked out at the men seated before him and asked,

"Now, tell me, what do today's readings mean to you?"

Several men shared personal reflections that touched me deeply. Then, one stood up and said,

"We, as religious ..."

It suddenly struck me that these men must all be priests! I had noticed a few wearing brown robes, but most of them were dressed in slacks or jeans. I later learned that I had stumbled into a Mass that was part of a month-long retreat. Some of the participants were priests, while others were seminarians. They had come from all over the United States to prepare for their solemn vows in the Franciscan order.

When the man finished speaking and sat down, the celebrant scanned the congregation one more time and asked,

"Does anyone else have anything to say?"

At that moment, as if propelled, my hand shot up in the air, probably to the disbelief of everyone present and certainly to me!

The priest acknowledged me and, feeling somewhat awkward, I said,

Marion Lee

"I don't know if I should be speaking here. I am the mother of seven children, and our youngest child has recently been diagnosed with an inoperable brain stem tumor. We have been praying through the intercession of Padre Pio, along with many other saints, for his miraculous healing, and I was wondering if I could ask for your prayers for our son, Kraig."

With that, each man assured me of his prayers. This spontaneous display of compassion touched my heart so deeply, my eyes began to tear. The Mass resumed, and the priest mentioned Kraig by name several times, petitioning God for a cure. At the Offertory, everyone was invited around the altar. I remained in my pew explaining that I had already attended an earlier Mass and had received communion. One of the men, in true Franciscan hospitality, came up to me and, with a warm smile, said,

"Our Lord has brought you to be in communion with us."

There I was, the only woman, the only non-religious, standing around the altar joined in prayer with all these holy men. It seemed almost dreamlike. At the Sign of Peace, one by one, each of them greeted me with a heartfelt promise to continue holding Kraig up in prayer. One seminarian, with a dark beard and wire-rimmed glasses, gently embraced me and said,

"My name is Jacques. I want you to know that

4

just before leaving for this retreat, I received word that my father has been diagnosed with an inoperable brain tumor. I ask you to pray for my father, and I will continually pray for the healing of your son."

It was such an astonishing coincidence, I stared at him in amazement, at the same time offering my prayers. Jacques later told me he was convinced that my presence in the chapel was an act of Divine Providence. There was no way I could possibly have known that at the very moment when I stood up and asked for prayers for Kraig, Jacques was deep in prayer for his father. The other Franciscans present were aware of his emotional struggle, and when I uttered the words *inoperable brain tumor*, they turned around to look at me and then immediately turned their gaze on Jacques.

When the Mass was over, I remained in my pew. Everyone left the chapel except Jacques, who walked back to where I was seated. I stood up, extended my hand and said,

"I'm Karyl Frick, and I am truly sorry about your father. Tell me, what is his name?"

"Fernand," Jacques replied.

"I will pray for a miracle for your father."

"I thank you for that," Jacques said, "and I thank you for reinforcing my hope. I was very distraught over my father's condition, yet I had not been praying for a miracle. I suppose I was too busy trying to accept the bad news."

I discovered that Jacques was from Canada, but his studies for the priesthood had taken him to the Washington Theological Union in Washington, D.C. He had just completed a year's internship at the Franciscan Chapel Center in Tokyo. Upon his return home, he discovered the critical nature of his father's illness. A cancerous, inoperable brain tumor had spread to the point where treatment would be useless. The doctor told Jacques that he should prepare himself because his father had a few months, at most, to live. Jacques was torn between staying at home to support his mother or attending the retreat at St. Malo's. His parents insisted that he go; they wanted nothing to interfere with his vocation. The decision was made easier by the fact that Jacques' brother took a leave of absence from his business in Montreal to return home.

I have no idea how long we stood there talking. Jacques' conversation was so riveting; it was as if time had been suspended. He was genuinely interested in learning all he could about Kraig and asked many questions. I wanted him to be able to put a face with the name when he prayed for Kraig, and it just so happened I had a photo with me. Fumbling through my purse for the picture, I dropped an envelope I was holding in my hand. The prayer cards it contained scattered all over the floor and Jacques bent down right away to retrieve them. His face took on an expression of disbelief as he lifted up a small card with a personal note from Sister Gabrielle Noel. Then he noticed a prayer to Marie of the Incarnation and a postcard bearing a picture of the Ursuline monastery in Quebec where she is buried.

"This is incredible," Jacques said, shaking his head. "We are praying to the same people! I received the call to my vocation at the tomb of Marie of the Incarnation, and the nuns from the Ursuline community in Quebec are personal friends of mine."

I explained to him that a friend of mine, an Ursuline nun, had asked me to pray for a miracle through the intercession of Marie of the Incarnation, a woman who is being considered for canonization in the Catholic Church. My friend wrote to Sister Gabrielle at the monastery requesting prayers for Kraig, and when she received a reply mentioning Kraig by name, she passed it on to me.

Striking a pensive pose, Jacques hesitated for a minute and then asked,

"Would it be possible for me to meet Kraig?"

A number of people had made the same request, but each time I had found myself having to politely refuse. My husband and I wanted to keep Kraig's life as normal as possible, and for Kraig, normal was being with family and close friends. Yet, I was so thrilled by Jacques' request, I didn't hesitate to ask him to come back to the cabin with me. Maybe it was the fact that we were sharing a similar cross, but I had a strong sense that inviting him was the right thing to do.

"I'll have to ask for permission," Jacques said, as we walked out of the chapel together. As I waited in the car, I realized that with all the excitement, I had forgotten to call my husband, Mike, to tell him the reason for my delay. He knew I had intended to make a visit, but it was well past the time when I should have been back. His sister, Maggie, was staying with us, and I was afraid they might worry needlessly.

Mike had good reason to worry. It wasn't all that long ago that I had a terrible accident right here in Colorado.

* * *

With seven children, life gets pretty hectic. You learn that vacations are not just a luxury, but a necessity. Mike and I place a high priority on getting away from it all. Ever since our honeymoon in Colorado, we had returned regularly during vacation periods with our ever-expanding family. Our dream was to one day have a place of our own. That dream came true the day we purchased a beautiful cabin nestled into the side of Deer Ridge Mountain in Allenspark. We signed the mortgage in November, but had to wait until the following March, when the younger kids were on break, to christen our mountain hideaway. Our two oldest,

Luke and Brian, were not able to join us at this time.

The spring air was still very cool as Mike and I and the children, with a U-Haul full of my parents' hand-me-down furniture, arrived at our cabin. Dry pine needles and twigs crackled under the tires as we pulled off the main route onto the dirt road that led to our vacation home. Mike had hardly pulled the key out of the ignition before all of us tumbled out of the station wagon. As I let the clean air fill my city-weary lungs, I found myself gazing at the picturesque backdrop to our cabin: the snow-capped mountains, dotted with pines, and the clear blue sky. "Heaven on earth," I whispered to myself, then I glanced over at Mike, who smiled back as if to say, "We did it!"

"This is going to be our best vacation ever," I thought.

Snowflakes were beginning to fall, and we worried about getting everything out of the trailer and into the cabin in time. Fortunately, it turned out to be a light dusting, nothing more. The first couple of days were spent cleaning up and arranging furniture. The kids pitched in and were so helpful that we promised to take them to a family restaurant nearby to mark the beginning of a real vacation. They jumped at the idea of a delicious hot meal with no dishes to wash. It's funny how I can look back and recall silly little things about that day. We had this waiter and the kids loved him. He was a distinguished elderly gentleman and the epitome of refinement. When he offered them free sherbet for dessert, the boys, all wide-eyed, looked at each other and in one voice shouted, "Yes!"

It was still early afternoon when I suggested we all go for a climb on the mountain behind our cabin. We were already very familiar with the mountain, having been in the area many times in the past. My proposal, however, did not meet with much enthusiasm from the weary band. Mike wanted to take a nap, Karl and Dan were engrossed in a video game, the girls were involved in other things, but Kraig, always ready for adventure, burst into the room.

"Mom, I'll go with you!"

"That's great, honey," I said. "We'll climb all the way to the top!"

I went out back to get the walking stick Mike had hewed from a large tree branch and smoothed out for me. I told Kraig he might want to bring a stick and also a jacket. It can get very cold as you reach the higher elevations. Our daughter, Ginger, was out on the back deck reading and soaking up some sun. With book in hand, she called to us and waved as we began our trek.

It wasn't a treacherous climb, though along the way we encountered some rugged spots. Kraig always sought out the more challenging route while I preferred a smoother path. As is usual on a mountain trail, when it gets a little tricky, you have to choose your own course. There were moments when Kraig and I were walking side by side, and other times when the terrain forced us some distance apart. Kraig was always within my sight, however, and we would meet again on level ground.

Kraig's exuberance knew no bounds.

"Mom, I can't wait to get to the top. This is really going to be cool."

His enthusiasm was contagious. I smiled back at him and all I could think of to say was, "Kraig, I love you."

The sun was radiant as we worked our way up the winding path. I started to feel quite warm. We stopped for a minute while I took off my sweatshirt and tied it around my waist. From our vantage point, we could see for miles. The panorama of pines below looked like a giant green carpet spread across the valley. Every time the cabin came into view, Kraig would shout,

"Mom, there's our roof, can you see it?"

Just below the summit, we came upon some patches of snow.

"Honey, come on over here! Let's write our names in the snow."

We took turns. Kraig went first. He took his stick with both hands and meticulously carved in the letters:

KRAIG

He was so proud of himself. I positioned my stick and wrote my name right next to his.

The top of the mountain wasn't much further, but by the time we reached it, we had been gone well over an hour. I turned to Kraig and said,

"You know, we better think about starting back. We don't want anyone to worry, and we want to get down before it gets dark."

As many know, heading down a mountain can be more challenging than climbing upwards. Tired knees wobble, and from a higher vantage point the path looks unfamiliar. I thought I was following the same route we had taken going up, but when you don't have an actual trail, it's easy to get side-tracked. Suddenly, the path became strewn with rocks and the going was rough. We were using our sticks, but at one point, I thought it might be better to let my stick slide to the ground just below, and pick it up when I got there. This was my plan, any-way. Down went the stick towards flatter ground; then, inch by inch, I made my descent. Kraig watched intensely from behind. Bracing my upper body on one of the large rocks, I could see my stick below, but between me and that safe place was a wide gap. I made a couple of false starts, but realized I wasn't able to stretch my leg far enough to find a safe footing. In literal terms, I was stuck between a rock and a hard place. I looked up at Kraig who had been anxiously watching my maneuvers.

"Honey, I'm not sure I can get to that spot below, and I don't think I can get back up to you, either. I'm a little worried."

Kraig looked right into my eyes and said,

"I'm worried too, Mom."

Whatever came next must have happened very quickly, because all at once, I was somewhere between mountain and sky. The last thing I remember before falling was the look of fear in Kraig's blue eyes ~ a look I had never seen before.

* * *

Jacques returned with a grin on his face. His superior had encouraged him to visit Kraig and spend some time with us. As he got into the car, I looked at my watch and turned to him saying, "You know Jacques, I was supposed to be home quite a while ago. I hope my family doesn't think I have fallen down the mountain."

He laughed, naturally thinking it was a joke.

"You may find this hard to believe, but sixteen months ago, I actually did fall off Deer Ridge Mountain!"

"You fell off the mountain?" Jacques asked incredulously.

"Yes, I did. Kraig was with me when it happened. I must confess, it is difficult to understand why God would spare me and then allow this horrible brain tumor to happen to Kraig. I still shudder when I think of how terrifying it had to be for him to watch me falling down a mountain. Kraig told me later that my body flipped a couple of times in mid air. He said it looked as if I were doing somersaults before I crashed onto a pile of rocks jutting out from the mountain."

"Was he able to get to you?" Jacques asked.

"Yes, but I was unconscious. Somehow ~ I don't know how ~ Kraig found his way to the bottom of the mountain, but in an area far removed from where we had begun our climb. There were no signs posted. I am convinced that the angels must have guided him back to the cabin."

"My husband, Mike, told me that when Kraig came through the door, he was out of breath and could barely speak. He told Mike that I had fallen and that I couldn't talk."

Jacques continued to listen with rapt attention.

"How long did it take Mike to find you?" he asked.

"Not too long. He immediately moved into action, instructing the kids to get flashlights and blankets. You know, he is wonderful in a crisis situation, and this was no exception. The six of them fanned out into groups of two and headed up to where Kraig led them. After searching for nearly an hour, our son Karl thought he heard something that sounded like weak moans. He came upon a clearing that led to the rocks where I lay, still unconscious. He called to Mike and the other kids to hurry and they all rushed to my side. When Mike saw the extent of my injuries, he asked Karl and Dan to run back to the cabin as fast as they could and call 911. Our property is in a remote area, quite a distance from the highway. After making the call, the kids had the presence of mind to run up to the highway to meet the ambulance. When Mike told me about this later, I was so very proud of them."

"The paramedics who arrived didn't waste any time. They realized my injuries were pretty severe and that they would need assistance getting me off the mountain. They radioed for more help and within an hour several teams, including the Rocky Mountain Rescue Team, were on the scene. They had to move quickly because it was beginning to get dark and the temperature had dropped down to the low thirties."

"How did they get you off the mountain?"

"They placed me in an inflated stretcher tied by belays. It took a team of three rescue units, coordinating their efforts, to get me off that mountain. I then had to be flown by helicopter to Denver General Hospital. I guess it created quite a ruckus in sleepy Allenspark with the blaring sirens, flashing lights, and a helicopter sputtering in the air. Of course, I saw or heard none of this."

"And the verdict?"

"Well, from the extent of my injuries, the doctors estimated I had fallen almost thirty feet. I had a fractured skull and concussion, as well as a broken shoulder, broken elbow, broken hip, and five separate fractures in my pelvis, not to mention the internal hemorrhaging."

Seeing Jacques wince, I attempted to interject some levity into the conversation.

"At the hospital, they allowed Mike and Ginger to stay with me while the other kids were taken to an empty waiting room. At one point, Mike wanted to talk to the doctor privately, so he said to Ginger, "Please stay in the room and take care of your mom. I'll be right back."

"As she stood over my bed looking down at tubes, bottles, and my badly bruised and still bleeding body, Ginger thought to herself, *Me? Take care of Mom?* She felt herself fading fast, and sure enough: Bam! She was out cold on the floor. The nurses ran into the room and placed her in the bed next to mine. When Mike drove the kids back to the cabin the next morning, they all had a good laugh about it. Believe me, they needed some comic relief after that horrible night."

Shaking his head while, at the same time, uttering a breathless *whew!* Jacques agreed. Then he asked, "How long was it before you were on your feet again?"

"Too long. I have to say that the accident, subsequent surgery, and a large part of my recovery are still a complete blur to me. The only memory I have of Denver is undoubtedly distorted by the painkillers I was on. I remember trying desperately to awaken from this horrible nightmare where I kept falling down a mountain. My eyes would open and close but it was impossible for me to stay awake. I was in such a state when I first saw Kraig's little friend, Rocky The Moose, lying next to me. Kraig did not want me to be alone in the hospital room, so he placed his little stuffed moose in my bed. There were many moments when I held onto that moose because it made me feel closer to the kids."

"I spent two weeks in Denver before being flown back to a hospital in Dallas where I spent two more weeks. My hip was a mass of shattered bones that the doctors had pinned together. They had no idea how long it would take to mend."

"It turned out to be a long and painful recuperation, the hardest part being the disruption of our family life. During this time, Karl was preparing for his confirmation, and Brian was getting ready to graduate from college. I was determined not to miss either event, even though everyone thought I was crazy to even think about it. Granted, it was difficult, but with Mike's support and a wheelchair, I was able to attend both celebrations. All the kids were wonderful throughout this ordeal, but I was particularly concerned about Kraig and what effect my accident might have had on him emotionally. He's a tough little guy, Jacques, but you'll soon see that for yourself."

As we were nearing the cabin, I cautioned Jacques to gently warm up to Kraig.

"By nature, Kraig is a very gregarious child; however, since the tumor and the medication, it's impossible to predict how he will react. I don't want to appear over-protective, but he is still a little boy and you, being a stranger... we don't want to frighten him."

"I understand completely," Jacques assured me.

The minute we arrived, my sister-in-law, Maggie, ran out to the car. She said Mike had gone out to search for me and was on the phone. I turned to look at Jacques.

"What did I tell you? He probably thinks I've had another accident!"

Maggie nodded her head affirming that was exactly what Mike feared. She said that Kraig and Dan were also very concerned. In fact, Kraig had asked her if she thought his mom had fallen off the mountain again. I felt terrible, and after introducing Maggie to Jacques, I ran in to take Mike's call. At the sound of my voice, Mike was greatly relieved. I told him I would explain everything later but to hurry home because we had a special guest.

I ushered Jacques into the living room where Kraig was curled up on the couch, his head resting on "Biggie," another member of Kraig's moose family. I explained to Kraig that Jacques really wanted to meet him because his father was also struggling with a brain tumor. In one brief glimpse, Jacques noticed an assortment of moose souvenirs in different places around the room. There were a couple of books with moose stories sitting on a table, and he even spotted an empty Moosehead Beer carton prominently placed on the mantle. That did it for Jacques! He came from an area that boasted of more moose than deer; in fact, Moosehead Beer is made in New Brunswick, the province where he was raised. It provided him with the perfect opening.

"Kraig, you must like moose almost as much as I do!"

Kraig's face lit up immediately.

"I come from moose country and I'll bet you can't make a moose call like I can."

The next thing I knew, Jacques pressed his hands against the back of his head, wiggled his fingers to imitate antlers, and broke into a symphony of moose calls. Kraig, giggling with delight, echoed the sounds right back at him. Dan heard these strange noises and ran downstairs to see what was happening. By the time Mike got back, Jacques had completely won over both of the boys. His magnetic personality and wonderful sense of humor made quite an impression on Mike, too. In fact, all of us were so completely at ease in Jacques' company, it was as if we had known him for years.

I pulled Mike aside to tell him again how sorry I was for not calling, and tried to describe what had taken place at St. Malo's. He couldn't resist the opportunity to tease me.

"Karyl, you're out of my sight for one minute and you pick up a Franciscan!"

We decided to go out for brunch and invited Jacques to join us. Kraig had already taken his medicine [steroids] and this meant he had to eat fairly soon. We all piled into the station wagon, squeezing Jacques in with us. At the restaurant, we were seated at a picnic table on the patio. The food took a long time getting to us. Kraig was feeling very hungry, and he let us all know it. Jacques, as if on cue, struck an appropriately sober pose and declared,

"You know, Kraig, if that food doesn't come out in the next few minutes, I am going to jump up on this table and do a dance!"

"You will? You really will?" Kraig asked with glee.

I warned Jacques that Kraig would hold him to

it. Just then, our food arrived and Jacques shot a glance at me, breathing a sigh of relief. I really believe that if it had been delayed one second too long, he would have danced on the table just to please Kraig.

Jacques is a man who captivates children with the charm of a "Pied Piper." I discovered, however, that there was also a deep, serious side to him. For one thing, his vocation came rather late in life. Jacques was already in his forties when we met him. Prior to joining the Franciscans, he was highly regarded as a community development professional, an author, and had traveled extensively around the world. There were so many facets to his personality, and he was such a brilliant conversationalist, that I could have listened to him all day.

While we were talking about the priesthood, I asked him when he first knew he had a calling. The circumstances of our meeting had already removed many barriers. Perhaps that explains why Jacques was willing to share an experience, so personal that he rarely talks about it. With arms folded, he reflected for a moment and then spoke.

"I was aware of the presence of God from the age of six. Believe me, I was not a pious child, but even at that tender age, I would find myself at school watching children in the playground and questioning whether or not they knew how near God was. I remember composing little prayers as a child, and I would hide them in different rooms throughout our house. When I entered college, a time when most kids put God on the *back burner*, I continued to remain faithful to the sacraments."

"Did your family help your vocation along?"

"You can't imagine how deep that question goes! I think I can say that my ancestry carved out my destiny. There had been a priest on our family tree in every generation going back to the seventeenth century, when my ancestors came over from France with the first bishop of "New France," which is now Canada. One of my ancestors was a porter for the bishop. So, you see, everyone knew that I, being the eldest son, would one day embrace my heritage. When I was fifteen years old, our pastor came for a visit to announce plans for sending me to a Redemptorist seminary. For my part, although I sensed God's hand on my life, I resisted total commitment. I wrote a long letter to the Redemptorists outlining all the reasons why I simply could not be a priest. To my great relief, they gracefully accepted my refusal."

"What got you on the road, then?"

Jacques slowly sipped his iced tea while pulling his thoughts together.

"It wasn't one single event, but rather, a series of experiences culminating in a life and death drama that finally propelled me into the seminary.

"I honestly believe the direction of my vocation began with an advertisement posted at the university I attended. Volunteers were being sought for a summer seminar in Haiti. The purpose was to have students go to a third world country to study the causes of poverty. For me, it was a purely academic decision, not missionary. I applied and was chosen, certainly not because I was bright or saintly. I was the *only* one who applied, and the only one stupid enough not to realize that Haiti was not about beaches and palm trees.

"After my arrival, I visited a clinic formerly run by a Canadian doctor and nurse, both of whom had returned to Canada. When they departed they left behind, of all things, a string of Christmas lights. The day before my arrival, a baby had been born prematurely in the clinic. There were no incubators. The nurse on duty had the ingenuity to wrap the string of Christmas lights around the baby. In essence, she saved the child's life. Seeing that tiny preemie surrounded by those colored Christmas lights ~ it changed my whole perspective on what life was about. I decided then and there that I had to do something for others.

"When I returned to the university, I volunteered to raise funds for clinics in Haiti. I worked through the auspices of World University Services of Canada (WUSC), the organization responsible for conducting the summer seminars. It was such a successful venture, I received a call from their office in Ottawa offering me a job. They wanted me to work on a national basis for campuses all over the country. I was working on my thesis at the time and this was an offer I couldn't refuse. I began working in international development, not realizing that God was laying the foundation for my future.

"After completing my post-graduate studies, I continued working for WUSC. I was twenty-seven years old, living in Ottawa, and carving out a career that was exciting and challenging. Everything was great except for the fact that I was constantly plagued with throat infections. When I finally went to see my doctor, he told me that my tonsils had to be removed. He was a nice, honest man, but he was in his seventies. I thought it prudent to seek another opinion. I made an appointment with a woman doctor whom I had never seen before. She turned out to be rough and tough ~ the type you might find in a motorcycle gang. I quickly decided, 'No, this will never do!' I set out once more and considered myself most fortunate to find a doctor who really made a good impression. He had a tastefully paneled office with beautiful pictures and fantastic, piped-in music ~ all the essential ingredients that go into making a fine surgeon . . . Right?!

"Needless to say, my standards were somewhat superficial and this folly nearly cost me my life. In performing the tonsillectomy, this surgeon apparently nicked my artery, though the accident wasn't discovered until I went home a few days later. I was sitting by myself, reading a book, when all of a sudden my throat was filled with blood. I immediately ran next door and asked my neighbor to take me to the hospital. By the time we arrived at the hospital, the bleeding had become profuse. I was having a massive hemorrhage!. They couldn't even give me a sedative. They just held me down on a steel bed and clamped the artery.

"During this procedure, my heart stopped . . . and I had what people call an *out-of-body* experience. It might sound funny, but I felt as if I was covered in flannel. As a child growing up in Canada, everything was made of flannel ~ my bedcover, my pillow, my pajamas ~ and, to me, this was a most comforting feeling. There was absolutely no pain. I was cradled in this wonderful feeling of warmth and surrounded by a tremendous light. Then, a presence came to me with an unmistakable message: **You can come over now, and that is fine, but I still have things to ask of you**. It was an indescribable voice ~ not audible ~ I felt it inside. The choice was mine to make and I chose to return to my body. When I opened my eyes, I looked into the face of a very startled nurse. The next day I pondered over every detail of the experience and finally came to the conclusion that the light and the voice must have been a dream. Yet, it had been so real! Then, the nurse who had been at my bedside confessed to me, in whispered tones, that during the panic, my heartbeat had suddenly become perfectly normal. It had to have been at the precise moment I decided to come back! She also told me that I was lucky to be alive. Her conversation was guarded for fear of repercussions for the doctor and the hospital."

"Sounds like a life-changing experience to me," I interjected..

"And then some!" replied Jacques. "Yet, I still did not recognize the call to the priesthood. I sincerely tried to be a better person, a better boss, a better friend to everyone. I knew I had a mission, but becoming a priest did not occur to me."

"Then, in 1989, God finally got my attention. I was staying at our family cottage in Maine, busy at work on my third book. As time wore on, I just didn't feel right. One day, I felt so ill, I laid down on my bed. The next morning, I felt worse. I couldn't hold anything down and started to spike a fever. As the fever raged on, totally out of control, I began to have convulsions and there was no question in my mind that I was indeed dying. A few years earlier, I had received a blood transfusion in Africa. The symptoms I was experiencing convinced me that I had contracted AIDS from tainted blood. It would just be a matter of time before someone found me dead in my bed. At one point, I was almost delirious with fever, thrashing my head back and forth on the pillow.

"On the wall directly above me, my eyes focused upon a huge crucifix. It was the original one that used to hang in the chapel in my hometown; before the Ursulines left the area, they had presented it to me as a gift.

"I struggled to sit up and, turning around, I stared into the eyes of Jesus on the cross and moaned: Jesus, I don't know what you want of me, but if you can take this pain and sickness away, I will say **yes** to anything you are going to ask. The instant I uttered my **yes**, it was as if a thousand tons had been lifted from my body. The pain vanished and the fever disappeared. I immediately fell on my knees and cried, "Lord, here I am." I returned to Canada and, within days, began looking into different religious orders. Thanks to God's grace, I found myself with the Franciscans."

I was mesmerized listening to this incredible odyssey which had led Jacques to the priesthood. Somewhat selfishly, I wanted him to stay with us for the entire day, but he had to return to St. Malo's.

Mike and I drove him back to the retreat center. When we got back to the cabin, we went for a long walk. Both of us marveled at my chance meeting with Jacques and what a blessing his visit had been for all of us, especially for Kraig. That evening, Jacques telephoned to thank us for a lovely day. Ironically, when he got back to St. Malo's, he also took a walk. He said he needed that time to be alone with the Lord. He also told me that in meeting us, he felt as though his life had turned not merely a "page" but a "chapter." Given the drama of his former life, I had no doubt that he was right and, quite frankly, was excited at the prospect of our being part of that new chapter. He hastened to add that he had been granted special permission to talk with us at any time of the day or night. This is highly unusual for one on retreat; however, under the circumstances, his superior felt Jacques might be of some help.

Jacques invited us to join him the following evening for Mass. Mike's sister had to return home in the morning but it just so happened that a close friend, Meg Fredrick, who also happened to be Kraig's godmother, would be arriving that afternoon. I knew she would want to come with us.

Meg had been our eldest son Luke's teacher in Junior High. She was having her first baby when our sixth one, Dan, was due. Meg still loves to tell the story about the day Dan was born. It was a day set aside for school conferences. In her finest professional manner, she was sitting across the desk from a concerned parent when the principal announced over the intercom that there was a message from Luke Frick. The next thing she heard was Luke's voice blaring, "Mrs. Fredrick, my mom just had a baby!" We laugh about it to this day.

I was thrilled that Mike and Meg would be able to share in the unique spiritual experience I had had at St. Malo's. As soon as the priest came out on the altar, he announced that the Mass would be offered for Jacques' father, Fernand, and our son, Kraig. What a powerful example of living faith it was to see these Franciscans, in unison, imploring God's healing mercy. It was an occasion we would hold dearly in our hearts.

The time spent with Jacques had been so extraordinary, I hardly knew what to say as we parted. Before I could speak, he handed me a holy card with a prayer of St. Francis of Assisi on it. He also gave me a package for Kraig and promised to keep in touch.

Kraig was thrilled when I presented him with Jacques' gift. He eagerly opened the box and pulled out a small, green, stuffed dog. There was also a card with a picture of an elk, and a note that read,

Kraig,

I hope this elk will do. I looked everywhere for a moose card but could not find one. The little dog in this box has always meant a lot to me and I want you to have it. I am keeping a special place for you in my heart and in my prayers.

Love,
Jacques.

Kraig had a special knack for choosing names. The green dog would be called Clover, but in keeping with family tradition, Kraig insisted it be Klover spelled with a "K."

It was comforting to know that we would be included in Jacques' prayers, but I had no way of knowing how deeply involved he would become in our lives.

Chapter II

A Time to Be Born (Eccles. 3:2)

I was born in St. Louis, Missouri and have always had an awareness of God's blessings, beginning with the wonderful parents who brought me to life. They were strong individuals with an unwavering faith that set a beautiful example for my brother and me. At that time, stay-at-home moms were the backbone of volunteer services, and my mother was a thoroughbred among volunteers. She was vivacious, had scores of friends, and was the heart of our home. Pop was a doctor, a family physician. I had great respect for my father because of his personal and professional integrity.

From early on, I thought about a future in medicine. Pop and I discussed the possibility of my becoming a doctor, but I knew that the demanding life of a physician would present too many conflicts with my other and greater desire to marry and have a large family. I decided that nursing would fit nicely into my plans. When the time came, I set my sights on Avila, a college for women in Kansas City, which offered an excellent four year nursing program.

Of Moose and Miracles

The first week at school, at a picnic for incoming freshmen, I met Mike Frick. He was a junior at Rockhurst, the nearby men's college. Right away, I was attracted by Mike's calm manner and practical approach to life. He was a perfect balance for someone like me whose reserved exterior served to disguise a somewhat emotional nature. It didn't take us long to figure out that our initial attraction was supported by shared convictions and dreams. The picnic led to our first date, which led to another, and by the time I was a senior, we were engaged to be married.

Our wedding took place in St. Louis at the Basilica of St. Louis, King of France (also known as the Old Cathedral). Like me, Mike loved and wanted children, but we never put a number on how many. We would just take them as God sent them along. For the first few years, Mike worked in Kansas City while I embarked on a nursing career. When I became pregnant with out first child, I put my professional activities on hold. Mike encouraged me to pamper myself and relax at home since I might not have such a luxury again for a long time. How right he was! Luke was born on April 2, 1971, followed two years later by Brian, and the year after that, Ginger. Then Klaire, Karl and Dan came in rapid succession. By the time Kraig arrived on the scene, Luke already had his driver's license.

With so many birthdays in our house, we early

on developed a family ritual that allowed some-one's big day to last from dawn to dusk. Early in the morning, before we go our separate ways, we gather together for the opening of cards and gifts. Then, in the evening, we celebrate with cake and ice cream. This tradition was well in place by September 9, 1987, Mike's birthday. That morning, the children and I were happily watching Mike open his birthday presents. I had to shift my position a few times to accommodate the as yet unknown member of the family who was due to make his public appearance a week later.

Before leaving for work, Mike turned to me and said,

"You were so quiet during my party this morning. Is everything O.K.?"

"Well, you just may have another present before this day is over!" I replied with a knowing smile.

Sure enough, Kraig Frick was born at 8:15 P.M. that night. Mike was thrilled with his "birthday present," and when Kraig was old enough to understand, he took special pride in sharing his father's birthday. I called them my "September the Ninth Guys" and it stuck.

Kraig's early arrival was just the first mani-festation of his vibrant personality. He brought such spark and pizazz to our family. A study in constant motion, he embraced life with inexhaustible energy. Kraig was *all boy* and seemed to know no fear. From the moment he learned to walk, he was literally off and running from one adventure to the next. He loved to climb. The expression "out of reach" had no meaning with Kraig around. In a matter of seconds, he could hoist himself up onto my kitchen cabinet, scoot down the counter, climb up on top of the refrigerator and get to the cupboard above.

Ever pushing the ceiling on his explorable universe, Kraig would often, fearlessly, toddle out of the house and into the yard. I remember one day, when Mike and I were weeding the garden, three year old Kraig made straight for the big wooden swing set. Before we had a chance to notice, he maneuvered himself onto the monkey bars. With his chubby little hands gripping the bars, he was suspended precariously between heaven and earth just as Mike and I turned our attention to him. Afraid to yell for fear he would drop, we moved with stealth and speed and caught him just in the nick of time. My heart was racing like a trip-hammer, but Kraig wasn't the least bit concerned. Back on the ground again, he headed for his next adventure.

Wherever he saw fun, Kraig just had to be part of it. On one occasion, the older children were laughing and splashing in the neighborhood pool, just having a grand time. Before we could stop him, Kraig was up on the diving board and into the water! He didn't even hesitate. He had decided what he wanted, and he went for it. That was Kraig all over.

I kept trying to think of ways to bring out a softer side. One idea I had was to put stuffed animals in his crib, but he wanted no part of them.

All our children, with the exception of Kraig, were very close to both my parents. My father became seriously ill while I was expecting Kraig and died a few years later. It saddens me that Kraig never really knew my father at his best. He was a super grandparent, interested in and involved with each child individually.

Pop had always been my hero, and his illness was my first real encounter with sadness. It came upon us with such suddenness. My parents had bought a condo in Florida to live out their golden years in style. While driving back to St. Louis, on his birthday, pop complained of a horrible pain down his back. The subsequent examination revealed that he had suffered a subdural hemorrhage and needed brain surgery. Pop remained in a coma for two months following his operation and the doctors were convinced he would not survive. In the meantime, I had delivered Kraig. I so desperately wanted my father to know Kraig that, as soon as I was able, about a month after delivery, I bundled up my baby and the two of us boarded a plane for St. Louis. Pop eventually recovered somewhat, but he never regained his former vibrancy and died five years later. Even though I could see it coming, his death was devastating for me.

Two years later, I lost mom. She suffered a heart attack while on the flight bringing her to Dallas to attend our son Luke's wedding. Lost in the chaos of last minute wedding details, I had sent Luke and Brian on ahead of me to meet the plane. By the time I arrived at the gate, the boys were pushing mom through the tunnel in a wheelchair. The airline officials wanted to take her to the hospital immediately upon landing, but she refused. As we maneuvered our way through the crowd, the idea occurred to me that I could swing by Medical City, where I knew the doctors, and have mom checked. I could hear her quietly praying the Hail Mary, so I whispered along with her. When we reached my car, Luke and Brian bent over to lift her from the wheelchair but she collapsed in their arms. We quickly called for an ambulance and mom was taken to the nearest hospital. The doctors in cardiac care told us there was really nothing we could do but wait. Meanwhile, we had the wedding rehearsal dinner that night and, of course, everything was set for the wedding the next day. Having done what we could for mom, we rejoined the family and prayed that the next twenty-four hours would be peaceful for her.

The wedding rehearsal came off without a hitch, and the ceremony the next day, though joyful, was nevertheless touched with a tinge of sadness by mom's absence. As I sat in the church with Mike at my side, I found myself caught up in the drama of life's cycles of beginnings and endings. Watching Luke clasp the hand of his bride, the memory of my mother clasping the beads of her rosary the day before permeated my thoughts. Mike and I kept in constant touch with the doctor throughout the day's activities, and the minute the reception was over, we rushed to mom's side where we passed a night of vigil. As the early morning sun announced a new day, my mother slipped away from us to enter eternal life. Mom died as she had lived, with a prayer on her lips. I honestly believe that the Lord, perhaps with some encouragement from His mother, kept my mother on earth just long enough for us to proceed with the wedding.

With the passing of my parents, and Luke's marriage to Regina, the Frick family opened another chapter in its history. We had been blessed by good health and touched by a minimum of sadness. With gentle pedagogy, God opened our hearts wider to live fully the gifts he had yet to give us.

Chapter III

A Time to Laugh (Eccles. 3:4)

With an age span of sixteen years between our oldest and youngest, the Frick household was always in high gear. There were endless timetables to be met: car pools, sports practices and games, dental appointments, plus the everyday ordinary chores necessary to keep things running smoothly. As the family grew, we certainly faced our fair share of challenges ~ it would be unrealistic not to expect problems along the way ~ but the joy of having a house full of children far outweighed any hurdles.

Our kids shared a competitiveness that made no allowances for age or size. Being the youngest, Kraig always seemed to try a little harder. He immersed himself so totally in everything he did, I had a real problem getting him down for naps. Kraig gave new meaning to the expression strong-willed child. I have always thought of myself as strong-willed, but I met my match in Kraig. It wasn't that he wanted to cross me ~ he simply did not want to miss out on anything. On those occasions when we locked horns, it was virtually impossible for me to stay angry. He was such a happy child and had an uncanny ability to make me laugh. I don't remember exactly how or when it started but, for years, Kraig and I had this special thing where I would say,

"Kraig, you make me . . ."

And, in a sing-song voice, Kraig would look me straight in the eye and shout back,

"Happy!"

I can still see those gorgeous blue eyes and that blond hair, bright as the sun, as he stood shaking his head amid peals of laughter. Such a simple thing, but it never failed to bring me joy.

Mike and I are great supporters of Catholic education. It has been our experience that parochial schools strive for excellence, and we have always set the bar high for our kids. The investment has meant making many sacrifices, but the dividends are already evident. Our children attended Mary Immaculate School from kindergarten through eighth grade. When they were ready for high school, the girls attended Ursuline Academy and the boys were enrolled in Jesuit College Preparatory School.

When Karl was a sixth grader, Kraig was in kindergarten. Most children that age are a little intimidated by upper classmen. Not Kraig! He would walk right up to a group of older kids and say,

"Hey, are you one of Karl's cool kid friends?"

Karl would nearly die of embarrassment and beg me to please make him stop, but Karl's friends thought it was great. When Karl was an eighth grader, he had one friend in particular, Matt, whom Kraig idolized. Matt was terrific in sports, and knowing how much Kraig looked up to him, he would shoot baskets and play ball with him as if he was just another one of the guys. They even had a secret handshake where they made all these goofy gestures. Baby brothers can really be a bother sometimes, but Kraig had a way of attracting friends in every age group.

Over the years, Mike and I came up with a variety of methods for maintaining peace within our brood. Long car trips sometimes tested our ingenuity. Inevitably, territorial disputes would ensue and these were settled only with novel diversionary tactics. Mike was a master at inventing on the spot road games like, "The first person to see a green jeep wins $1.00." For the big money, the stakes were much higher: "The first person to see a truck with Alaskan plates, carrying a boat with three goats in it, wins $5.00!" Fortunately, these games usually restored peace, at least temporarily.

Some of our most memorable car trips were a little bit crazy. Like the time we were cruising down the highway and suddenly Mike became very agitated. I asked him what was wrong and he said,

"Do you see that car behind me? That guy has been on my bumper for ten miles."

"Just let him pass," I suggested.

Mike slowed down and the car pulled up alongside us. The man behind the wheel had been desperately trying to get our attention to tell us that a suitcase had flown off the top of our nine passenger station wagon. You would think with all of us in the car someone would have seen or heard something! We had two very large suitcases plus some canvas bags tied to the luggage rack. One of the suitcases was filled with clothes for the five younger children. The other one belonged to Mike and me and had all our clothes and toiletries inside. Neither of them had any identifying tags. After checking the top of the car and discovering that the missing case was ours, I had this sinking feeling, certain that our clothing was strewn all over the interstate! Mike immediately turned around, and with our noses pressed against the windows, we all scanned the highway for several miles but saw no evidence of the suitcase or its contents. We checked in at a few truck stops and even notified the highway patrol on the off chance that someone may have retrieved it. A month later, the mystery of the missing suitcase was solved. Our pharmacist received a call from a man in California who had found the case. The man had discovered a bottle of medicine tucked into one of the corner pockets and was able to trace us through the pharmacy. From that day on, no matter how crowded we were, all luggage went inside, or it didn't go at all!

If I had to pick a favorite time with the family, it would probably be Christmas. I love everything about the holidays, from baking cookies to trimming the tree. Selecting a tree is a ritual that requires the presence of each family member. The trick is to find one big enough to satisfy everybody, at the same time making sure it will fit through the door! Over the years, we have had some spectacular trees, but there is one that will forever be etched in my memory.

It was two weeks before Christmas. We had all happily agreed on a huge blue spruce tree which Mike and the older boys fastened to the top of the station wagon. On the way home, we pulled into a gas station. In Texas, a complimentary car wash used to accompany a fill-up. Never one to turn down such an offer, Mike circled the car around. The kids were hyped up about the holidays, and with so much chatter and laughter in the back of the car, we had completely forgotten that the tree was on the roof! Despite the roar of sloshing water reverberating from every direction, raucous laughter could be heard emanating from the line of cars behind us. (Feel free to start singing, "In the lane, soap was glistening . . .")

One particularly precious Christmas moment took place when Kraig was six years old. There definitely was a softer side to Kraig, and that

Christmas I tapped into it quite by accident. With a few last minute gift items on my list, Klaire, Ginger and I set out for Macy's. The sweet scent of pine and bayberry filled the air as we browsed through different departments admiring all the holiday ornaments and glitter. I was standing at one of the counters when my eye caught sight of a seasonal promotion. If you spent a certain amount, for just a few dollars more, you could buy a cute little moose. This soft, cuddly creature, all decked out in a green scarf, was so adorable it just captured my heart. Holding it at arm's length, I pondered the possibility of presenting it to Kraig from Santa.

"Forget it, Mom," Klaire said, reading my mind. "You know Kraig won't appreciate a stuffed animal."

"It doesn't matter how cute it is, he won't like it!" chimed in Ginger.

I knew the girls were right, but my first impulse proved to be irresistible. I yielded and bought the moose. On Christmas morning, I perched him atop a present under the tree, with a note to Kraig from Santa.

It was love at first sight! Kraig dubbed his furry little friend, "Moosie," and from that day on, they were inseparable. Kraig never once thought of Moosie as an inanimate stuffed toy. Moosie was as real to him as any human.

The next year, before Christmas, I took Kraig

to visit Santa. In the car on the way, I asked him what he wanted for Christmas.

"Mom," he said, "I just don't know what I want, but Moosie really needs a friend. Would it be okay to ask Santa if he could bring a friend for Moosie, and maybe just a few toys for me?"

It was one of those precious, poignant moments moms live for.

"Yes, Kraig, that would be just fine."

Later, I watched him sitting on Santa's lap, as serious as could be, explaining how Moosie needed a friend. I think even Santa was impressed. In any case, *Rocky the Moose* arrived Christmas morning. He was smaller than Moosie and dressed in a green ski jacket, with a plaid hunter's cap on his head and a matching scarf. It was always *Rocky the Moose* ~ no nicknames would do. Kraig gave a lot of serious thought in choosing names. It couldn't be just any old name; it had to have a purpose. Rocky the Moose was so named because of Rocky Mountain National Park in Colorado where we had spent a lot of time.

The next moose to join the clan was Parky. While we were on vacation, we took the kids shopping. All of the children had their own money to spend, and Kraig said he wanted to buy another moose. We were in one shop watching the kids rummage through aisles of souvenirs when Kraig saw his moose. It was wedged between other items on a shelf, completely out of reach for him, and so tiny I couldn't believe that Kraig had spotted it at all. It sported a blue T-shirt with Estes Park, Colorado printed on it in white letters. Hence, Kraig derived the name "Parky."

The moose family now numbered three, but like their host family, the Fricks, they continued to multiply. Kraig coined the name "Magic Moose," and he most emphatically did not welcome any remarks about his stuffed animal collection. His Magic Moose were real! They had personalities, histories, likes and dislikes, dreams and fears. They could not be passed over or forgotten. The moose were included in many family activities and always came on family vacations. It was difficult sometimes to fit them in the car, especially when all nine of us were together, but I never had the heart to suggest that Kraig leave any of them at home ~ it would have been tantamount to leaving one of the kids behind.

No one, including myself, could have imagined the attachment Kraig would develop for these Magic Moose or how, through his innocent eyes, every one of us would come to see the Moose Family as part of our own.

Chapter IV

A Time To Weep (Eccles. 3:4)

We taught our children the basic fundamentals of reading before they were enrolled in school. When I began to work with Kraig, however, he just wasn't picking it up. I was a bit concerned. The other children were very bright and had done well in school. What could be the problem with Kraig? After a few rounds of tests, it turned out that Kraig was dyslexic. But Kraig wasn't going to let anything hold him down for long. By the time he reached the second grade, he was at the top of his class. His above average intelligence and desire to excel in everything enabled him to compensate for the difficulties of dyslexia.

Participation in sports has always been a *given* with our kids. They made their first appearance in the bleachers as infants in my arms, and later could count on the family cheering section as they took to the field. Kraig was a natural athlete, and his proficiency in sports was fine-tuned early on by playing with his older brothers and sisters. Before he was school age, we enrolled him in gymnastics ~ a wonderful outlet for all that bottled-up energy.

When Kraig was old enough for team sports, he excelled in baseball, soccer and swimming, winning first place trophies and ribbons.

Mike and I were faithful and enthusiastic fans, but on those occasions when scheduled games overlapped, we had to attend separate events. The important thing is we made every effort to be there for all the kids, and up until the time of my accident, things worked out fairly well. During the time I was confined to a wheelchair, our son, Brian, filled the gap for me. After college and before accepting a job in Boston, "Bri" stayed home for several weeks to help out. It fell on him to take my place at sporting events. He also drove me back and forth to therapy and helped to carpool the kids to school.

After my accident, it took almost a year to get back into a normal routine. I had taught childbirth classes one night a week at the hospital. It afforded me the opportunity to keep my hand in nursing and gave me enormous pleasure. The young, expectant moms delighted in the fact that I was the mother of seven with enough experience to answer their endless supply of questions about parenting. When I was finally able to resume teaching, it was a great personal victory for me.

The Christmas following my accident was especially joyous, not the least of which was being able to participate in the festivities. This was the Christmas Biggie arrived. Kraig took one look at this moose, larger than all the others put together, and shouted,

"I am going to call him Biggie!"

Kraig loved every moose in his menagerie, but this one was special. I can still see him running in the house after school and snuggling up next to Biggie. With a sparkle in his eyes, he would look up at me and squeal,

"Mom. Biggie is the best!"

I would nod my head in agreement and add,

"Yes, Kraig, and you're the greatest!"

It was shortly after the holidays that Kraig started having a few problems. In the beginning, they were isolated incidents, not serious enough to warrant concern.

One day at school, he got sick and his teacher called me. At the time it happened, Kraig was attending Ash Wednesday Mass with his class. His teacher tried to persuade him to eat something, thinking perhaps that the day of fasting had been too much for him. It was true that Kraig had been fasting, but this was his own doing. He was trying to emulate his big brothers and sisters. He was also preparing to make his First Communion and was taking religious matters very seriously. He got sick at school a couple more times, but there was no discernible pattern, making it difficult to pinpoint the problem. The school would call me, I would drive over to pick him up, but as soon as he saw me, he would be okay.

One morning, Kraig wanted to know if he could take Biggie to school. Not quite sure how to handle such a request, I asked if he had discussed it with his teacher.

Kraig was a big, tough kid and the last thing he would want would be someone saying, "Look at him ~ he has a stuffed animal!" Yet, he was so insistent that I finally told him to ask for permission. That afternoon, Kraig was happy to report that his teacher agreed to allow Biggie to come to school the next day.

"We'll have to make sure Biggie gets dressed in a school uniform just like the other children," I told him.

Kraig was elated, and his classmates loved the fact that a moose was in the classroom. I think it was the uniform!

The next turn of events happened one afternoon while Kraig was sitting across from me in the kitchen doing his homework. I had enough experience to know that boys could be rambunctious without the slightest provocation, but I was surprised when Kraig leaned on the back of the chair and suddenly tumbled onto the floor. Ordinarily, he had such a wonderful sense of balance. It was completely out of character for him to fall like that. And, more peculiarly, when he got up, he was holding his left arm in a very strange way. Then, his left leg began trembling. I reached over and gently placed my hand on his knee.

"Honey, why are you shaking your leg?" I asked.

"I don't know, Mom," he answered.

Patting his knee, I whispered,

"Just see if you can calm down."

"Mom, I'm real tired," he said.

"Why don't we finish your homework," I suggested, "and then you can hop into my bed and take a nap."

Before leaving for the hospital to teach my class, I called Mike to discuss the incident with him. Kraig had a soccer game scheduled later that evening and we agreed that if he felt all right, there was no reason for him not to play. I told Klaire to let him sleep until dad got home.

Call it maternal instinct, but before leaving the hospital, I had to call home to see how Kraig was feeling. Mike told me that when he got home, he had had a tough time waking Kraig up. Once they got to the field, Kraig's behavior continued to be unusual. A normally scrappy, aggressive soccer player, Kraig got on the field and could barely walk without difficulty. He was favoring his left leg and arm. The coach could not understand what was happening and finally had to remove him from the game. Mike thought it might be the flu, but there was no evidence of fever. By the time they got home, the only complaint Kraig had was that he was tired.

The next day, Kraig wanted to go to school, so I didn't resist him. He ran off to his car pool, but during the ride complained of a headache and pain in his stomach. He got sick in the car. I rushed over to school with some fresh clothes, and once again, when he saw me, he was fine.

I had a long talk with Kraig's teacher. We discussed the fact that some children cannot express their inner fears or feelings; often times, this is manifested in stomach problems or other psychosomatic difficulties. She had an intuitive sense that something was wrong with Kraig. For this reason, she had allowed him to bring Biggie to class, hoping it might help whatever it was that was bothering him. The school nurse, who was familiar with all of our children, commented on the fact that none of our kids had ever gone to her office unless they were really sick. It baffled her that Kraig seemed to improve the moment I arrived on the scene.

Some of our friends had suggested that perhaps Kraig's behavior was a delayed reaction to my accident. What may have prompted this notion was the fact that we were making preparations to return to Colorado for the first time since my fall. All the injuries I had sustained were on my left side: the peculiar symptoms flaring up in Kraig were all on his left side. Adding to this his on again/off again stomach problems and you had a good case for assuming the foundation was psychological. In fact, our pediatrician had warned us to be aware of such a possibility. Even though it was a real stretch for Mike and me to believe all this, we had to wonder if Kraig was showing evidence of trauma.

There were other signs, but again, nothing consistent. They would vanish as suddenly as they appeared. For instance, sometimes Kraig's speech pattern would change in the middle of a sentence. We also noticed that on a few occasions he was drooling, but the minute we confronted him, he would stop. Reacting to Kraig's behavior became a delicate balance between firmness and sensitivity. If he was merely trying to get attention, we didn't want to over-react; at the same time, we could not ignore a cry for help. Our difficulty was exacerbated by the fact that Kraig never complained of pain.

Neither of us was prepared for what would soon unfold.

We were to leave for Colorado on March 8. It had been one year since my fall. If Kraig was suffering from an emotional problem, maybe going back to the cabin and facing the mountain again might alleviate his anxiety. We decided to do our best to keep him occupied with lots of fun things to do.

A few days after our arrival, we invited some neighbors over. While we were visiting with this couple in the dining room, the kids were busy in the living room gobbling down the snacks I had prepared for them. Without any warning, Kraig began to choke. I tried to apply the Heimlich maneuver, but I lacked the strength in my left arm. Mike ran in, grabbed Kraig, and was able to dislodge a chunk of food. While this event was upsetting, we did not connect it with the other things that were happening.

We had a big snowfall that night, so the next day we decided to go skiing. A few of the kids had been on skis before, but it wasn't a sport any of them had seriously pursued. We are a family of hikers, not skiers. But, since there was a lot of snow on the ground, we thought we'd give it a try. Because of the injuries from my accident, I was going along strictly as a spectator.

While Mike was standing in line to buy the tickets for the lift, I could see that Kraig was apprehensive. After a while, he turned to me and said,

"I don't know if I can do this or not."

"Kraig, if you don't want to ski, you can sit with me in the lounge. We'll have some hot chocolate and watch Dad and the kids try to tackle the slopes."

He was struggling to make a decision but

finally ran over to Mike and said he wanted to join them. In the lodge, I sat close to a window to get a good view. Kraig fought as hard as he could to stay up on those skis, but he kept falling. With every spill, I tried to rationalize in my own mind that it was because he had never been on skis before; deep down inside, I had an uneasy feeling.

On the drive back to the cabin, something happened that forced me to finally face my fears. Kraig wanted to take some pictures of a blue spruce for a school project. Despite his age, he was normally quite adept with a camera; in fact, we had been amazed at the quality of some of his early photos. This day, however, something was definitely wrong. Try as he might, Kraig simply could not focus the camera. It was frustrating for him, and just as difficult for us to watch. Afterwards, he fell asleep in the car, and like before, it was a deep sleep.

As a nurse, I have the training and experience to recognize the signs of a serious illness. In this case, however, I wasn't just a nurse ~ first and foremost, I was a mother. I didn't want to think about the possibility that something could be wrong with Kraig. With all the courage I could muster, I turned to Mike and whispered,

"I wonder if Kraig has suffered a stroke?"

I desperately wanted him to disagree with me. Instead, he said,

"I'm really concerned, too. Something is wrong."

As soon as we reached the cabin, I called our pediatrician's office and told him everything I could think of that might be important. Carefully choosing his words so as not to alarm me, he said he would set up an appointment for the following Monday with a pediatric neurologist. We left Colorado on Saturday and drove straight through to Dallas. Kraig slept for most of the trip. When we got home, I asked Mike if we should take him to the hospital right away instead of waiting until Monday. Mike looked at me seriously and said,

"I promise we will do the right thing. For now, let's get a good night's sleep, and we'll see where we are in the morning."

When morning came, we rose early and got everyone ready for Mass. As we were entering the church, the other kids went on ahead while Mike and I walked hand-in-hand with Kraig. It just so happened that my doctor and his wife (who are personal friends of ours) were walking behind us. After observing Kraig, they both became concerned. Before entering the church, they pulled me aside and asked what was wrong. When I explained the situation, they asked why I wasn't at the emergency room right then.

"I need to be here at Mass," I whispered.

"We'll sit close by in case you need any help,"

they assured me.

Before leaving the house, we had told the children we would take them to brunch when Mass was over, but after Communion, Mike and I decided not to wait a minute longer to take Kraig to the hospital. Naturally, he was upset, insisting that he wanted to go out to eat like we had promised. Mike slid his arm around Kraig's shoulder and in a soothing voice explained that we would see what the doctor had to say, and then we'd go to brunch. That seemed to satisfy Kraig. Our friends had agreed to drive the other kids home, so we quietly got up and slipped out of the church.

Mike dropped Kraig and me off at the emergency room entrance and went to park the car. We no sooner got inside when I heard the words:

Triage him immediately![1]

A feeling of dread smothered me as I held onto Kraig's hand. The next thing I knew, we were guided into a private room, and before long, a neurosurgeon came in to examine him. He instructed the staff to order a battery of tests, and then I heard him say,

"We'll need a CAT scan."

Mike was once again at my side. Our immediate concern was to protect Kraig from being frightened, so we called Luke and told him to go

---

1 Triage is a medical term referring to the priority of a patent's treatment.

over to our house, get Biggie, and bring him to the hospital as soon as possible. A short time later, Luke and his friend Steve showed up, each bearing a moose. Luke had Biggie, and Steve brought Moosie.

Things were happening so quickly, we scarcely had time to react. Mike and I were permitted to stay close by Kraig during the CAT scan. Afterwards, when I saw them put a Heparin lock in Kraig's arm, I turned to Mike and cried,

"My God, they're going to do brain surgery on our baby!"

At that point, we were ushered into a room filled with doctors and nurses. One of the doctors came over and asked us to sit down.

"I am afraid we have bad news," he said. "Your son has an inoperable brain stem tumor . . ."

I felt as if a knife had gone through me. All I could do was repeat over and over,

"Oh my God, Oh my God!"

I squeezed Mike's hand as hard as I could. It was an awful scene. Then, one by one, the medical staff walked out of the room to give us a chance to be alone. There was nothing either of us could say. We were stunned and grief stricken. We held on to each other and dissolved into tears. When we were able to pull ourselves together, we approached one of the doctors and asked if there could be any other possibility. He said there was a slim chance that Kraig was suffering from a bacterial infection. Mike and I clung to that small thread of hope. In the morning, an MRI would be done to confirm or deny the initial diagnosis.

With all of this going on around him, Kraig's big concern was missing brunch. He did not want to stay in the hospital because it meant he would miss out on the restaurant. I went to one of the doctors and asked,

"How about if we just take him home and come back first thing in the morning?"

"I would not recommend that," the doctor replied. "Kraig could develop Hydrocephalus."[2]

I heard myself crying, "What will I say to my child? What will I tell him?"

A nurse on staff spoke up and said,

"Tell him the truth. Tell him he has a lump in his head that causes him to stumble."

With all the courage I could muster, I walked back to the room where Kraig lay and told him exactly what the nurse had said. Then, I explained that the doctor wanted him to stay a while longer. I promised Kraig we would go home as soon as possible and we would definitely go to brunch.

---

2 Hydrocephalus refers to an abnormal increase in the amount of fluid in the cranial cavity, causing enlargement of the skull, especially the forehead, and atrophy of the brain.

"Right now, honey, they want to give you a special medicine to stop the swelling that is surrounding the lump in your head," I said.

After settling Kraig into a private room, Mike left for home. He realized how important it was to sit down with the kids and explain everything to them. Meanwhile, I walked Kraig down the hall to the playroom. There were other children in the room and they invited him to join them in playing bingo. He was so excited because he kept winning, and despite the torment I was feeling inside, I had to keep smiling.

The hospital chaplain had notified our parish priest, Father Gray, and he came as soon as he could. During Father Gray's visit, a nurse came in the room with a glass of Seven-Up for Kraig. This created a big problem. Kraig called all soft drinks "Coke," and he had given up Coke for Lent. Upon hearing this, Father Gray laughed and said,

"Seven-Up is not Coke, Kraig, and that means you can drink it!"

"Are you sure?" Kraig asked.

"I'm absolutely sure," Father Gray promised, marveling at Kraig's concern to be faithful to a promise made to God.

Father Gray and I had a chance to speak privately in a room down the hall. Together, we knelt down and said the Lord's Prayer. When we came to the part, "And deliver us from evil," I kept repeating those words again and again. As he was getting ready to leave, I said,

"You know, Father, Kraig was preparing to make his First Holy Communion. It's so important to him. . . and to me. I don't know now if he will be able to be with his class when the time comes."

"Don't worry, Karyl," Father Gray assured me. "Kraig will make his First Communion, if not with his class, then I will come to your home and administer the sacrament."

Father Gray's promise was our only consolation that day ~ a day when our whole world had been turned upside down. Every time I stepped outside of Kraig's room, I gave in to my sorrow and let the tears flow like a baby. Then, I braced myself to go back. I wiped my eyes dry, put on a smile, and returned to my son's side. I wouldn't increase his suffering by even the slightest hint of my grief.

I'll never forget one of the nurses warning me to be prepared because, sooner or later, Kraig was going to ask me about dying and I would have to answer him. I didn't know what to say to her. I muttered something about my Catholic faith and the idea of eternal life. The nurse's statement had completely taken me back. Speaking to my baby about death. . . I tried not to think about it, but the question kept nagging me. What would I say when the moment came?

Phone calls still had to be made to two of our

children, Ginger and Brian. As soon as Brian heard, he made plans to fly in from Boston the next morning. Ginger was in Mexico with a group of school friends, but she returned home on the next plane. I also called Kraig's teacher to let her know he would not be in school the next day. She dropped everything and came right over to the hospital. Kraig was delighted when his teacher said she would come back with work for him so that he could stay on track. Attending to details like this helped us to get through this awful day.

Mike and I stayed overnight at the hospital. The MRI was scheduled for early morning. What little sleep I got was fitful. My mind kept tracing scenes from Kraig's life. At one point, I was overwhelmed by the memory of something Mike had said to me while I was recovering from my fall. He said that we really had to enjoy every moment we are given because you never know what the future holds. Like an echo, those words kept swirling in my mind as I lay there fighting gruesome images of what might lie ahead for my child. I prayed, I cried, and I prayed some more.

The results of the MRI were certain and devastating. Kraig had an inoperable brain stem tumor. After receiving the dreadful news, Mike and I were asked to participate that evening in a conference with a group of doctors to discuss a treatment plan for Kraig. When we arrived at the meeting, we were gratified to discover a former neighbor and friend, a radiologist, among the doctors. Another personal friend, a pediatric neurologist, had heard the news about Kraig and came to the hospital just to be with us for moral support. He would not be involved medically with Kraig, but his presence was a great comfort because he was able to ask intelligent questions on our behalf and explain the answers in layman's terms.

Nonetheless, the meeting was emotionally draining. A course of treatment was laid out for us, but it offered precious little hope. Kraig would be discharged from the hospital and placed in the care of a radiologist and a pediatric oncologist. Steroids coupled with radiation and chemotherapy would keep the pain in check and buy some time. Nothing more than that could be done.

When the meeting drew to a close, I turned to our friend the neurologist and sighed,

"We have not heard one word of hope here tonight. Are there ever any miracles?"

"Yes," he said. "There are cases beyond our capability that have a good ending, and none of us can say why."

His admission reminded me that doctors are mere mortals, and God can and sometimes does perform miracles.

Later, I formulated my own "treatment" plan. I wanted every angel and saint in heaven, and every person I could enlist on earth, to pray for a miracle cure for Kraig. I began marshalling my forces that very night. With every phone call that had to be made, and every repetition of the desperate facts, I also pleaded for prayers.

Chapter V

A Time to Seek (Eccles. 3:6)

Kraig remained in the hospital for two days. Chemotherapy would be done on an outpatient basis at Children's Hospital and radiation would be administered at St. Paul's. The oncologist told us that, in Kraig's case, it really didn't matter if the tumor was malignant or benign. It was the location that presented the problem. The brain stem controls all of one's vital functions. A benign tumor can do as much harm as a malignant one.

I had not used the words tumor or cancer when I explained to Kraig that he had a lump in his head. My futile attempt to protect him was over once we entered St. Paul's. A huge sign greeted us: ST. PAUL'S CANCER CENTER.

Dr. Louis Munoz, the radiologist who had participated in the conference at Children's Hospital, would be part of the team working with Kraig at St. Paul's. A series of appointments were set up for Kraig, the first of which would be in a few days. Without going into great detail, I wanted somehow to prepare my son for what lay ahead. I told him truthfully that some of what the doctors had in mind was going to be hard, but I promised him that we would take every other moment we had to have fun. He accepted my words and took what came to pass in stride.

Nothing, however, could have prepared either one of us for the horror of radiation. With a moose tucked under one arm, and the hand of his other arm in mine, Kraig and I entered the stark X-ray room together. While the technician was busy getting Kraig ready, I placed the moose in a chair over in the corner, making certain it was visible to him. There was barely enough time to say, "I love you," before I had to leave my little boy strapped down on that cold table all by himself.

As the treatments progressed, other patients in the waiting room, all there for one cancerous reason or another, became quite smitten with Kraig. They always made a fuss over him and whatever moose he happened to have with him that day. When Kraig's treatment was finished, he did not want to linger for one second longer than necessary. The other patients understood and were not the least bit insulted if he rushed past them without so much as a "good-bye."

The confrontation that I had been dreading more than anything finally happened one day while Kraig and I were driving down the street on our way to the hospital. Kraig suddenly burst out with,

"Mom, what if I die early?"

So there it was. No matter how many times a scenario like this had come to mind, I was never able to find the right words. I believe now that what I told Kraig came directly from the Holy Spirit. Very calmly, I answered him,

"Honey, none of us knows when we are going to die. I can't promise you that a car isn't going to come out of nowhere, hit us head-on, and kill both of us today. But I promise you one thing: you will not die one moment before nor one moment after God calls you to be with Him."

I could see Kraig in the rear view mirror, so serious, as he looked straight ahead, then said,

"It's kind of scary, isn't it, Mom?"

I felt as though my insides were coming apart. I clutched the steering wheel tightly, took a deep breath, and said,

"Yes, Kraig, it's kind of scary."

Looking back, I have to say that during these days we never felt alone. Friends rose to the occasion and did everything possible to ease our burden. Dr. Steve Crow, our pediatrician, went so far as to give me his hospital parking pass. This was an enormous help, especially as time went on and Kraig's mobility became more impaired. I remember one day in the hospital parking lot; I had just reached back into the car to get Moosie, when I turned around to find Steve standing in front of me.

"I'm going to push this wheelchair today," he said.

The next thing I knew, he was zipping Kraig up and down the halls of the hospital, all the while keeping a running conversation. Here was a doctor who took the time to be a friend in a place that can be terribly frightening for a child.

My plea for prayer spread swiftly among family and friends, and, before long, people I didn't even know were joining our ranks to beg God for a miracle. One woman, whose prayers were very powerful, came to us indirectly through Meg, Kraig's godmother. She had prevailed upon a close friend of hers from Minnesota to pray for Kraig. This friend, in turn, took the request to her rosary prayer group and, after a few weeks, called me personally to ask about Kraig. During our conversation she said,

"I don't know what your feelings are about locutionists. . ."

I had to interrupt.

"Lo . . . What?"

I had never heard the word before. She explained that a locutionist is a person who receives inner messages. She went on to describe the leader of their prayer group, a woman who received such messages from Jesus and the Blessed Mother while she was in prayer. Because many people had experienced healing through this woman's intercession, she had told her about Kraig. The locutionist wanted to talk to Mike and me personally. Evidently, this was an unusual gesture since she did not normally seek out people who were added to her prayer list. Although this was uncharted territory for me, I was excited. Even Mike, ever the practical one, embraced the idea in good faith. We made the first contact by phone. With a soft, soothing voice that calmed our troubled hearts, she advised us to place ourselves in the presence of God by going to adoration with Kraig as soon as possible, and assured us that the Blessed Mother's mantle was over our family. This first phone call was just the beginning. We began corresponding. One day, I received a letter from her on small, cream colored stationery. In the upper left-hand corner was a picture of a large teddy bear holding a book in his lap entitled *Bears*. The cover on the book showed the face of another bear wearing a black jacket, white collar and a big red bow. As I gazed at the letter, I could hardly believe my eyes. I had cross-stitched a blanket with the identical bear-holding-the-book picture while I was expecting Kraig! For me, this was further confirmation of God's intervention in our lives.

Our hope rested on Divine intervention, but we saw no evidence of any change as we moved forward with plans for Kraig's First Holy Communion. Reception of the sacrament was scheduled to take place at All Saints Catholic Church, on April 14, during the 9:15 A.M. Mass.

Thanks to Father Gray, Kraig would receive communion privately in our home later in the day.

Early in the morning, Mike helped me to plant a rose garden. Ever since I began to include St. Therese (The Little Flower) in my morning devotions, roses have taken on a whole new meaning for me. One of the traditional prayers I use is: "Oh Little Therese of the Child Jesus, please pick for me a rose from the heavenly gardens and send it to me as a message of love." I even stepped out in faith and began to ask that she send me a sign. With God's grace, perhaps a profusion of heavenly blooms would soon appear in our backyard, a sign from St. Therese that Kraig was being healed.

April 14 also happened to be Divine Mercy Sunday. Weeks earlier, a woman from our parish, having heard about Kraig, came to the house with a book explaining the Divine Mercy devotion and special novena that begins on Good Friday and culminates the Sunday after Easter. Even though Mike and I had completed the novena and were busy preparing for Kraig's First Communion, I still managed to slip away to the Divine Mercy closing prayer service. It took place at 3:00 P.M., the hour of our Lord's death on the cross. When I stood up to leave the church, I felt someone tap me on the shoulder. It was Bridget Toro, our parish cantor. She handed me some prayers to the Italian stigmatist, Padre Pio; it was the first I had ever heard of him. Bridget told me she was praying for Kraig's miracle cure through the intercession of Padre Pio. I thanked her for the prayers and rushed home.

When I arrived, I found everything ready. Kraig's First Communion banner, the one he would have presented at Mass had he been able to receive with his class, was draped over the mantle. I placed some fresh flowers on the hearth, which added a lovely touch. Even though Kraig had completed all the sacramental instructions and was well prepared, he was inordinately nervous. It was a cruel reminder of how the brain tumor was affecting his personality. The other reminder was not nearly so subtle. Kraig's beautiful features were becoming distorted by the increased swelling, a result of taking steroids. None of his clothes fit anymore; even the pants we had recently bought for him were already snug.

By the time Father Gray arrived, Kraig was a bit more relaxed, and after chatting for a while, he was completely at ease. Father told us that the children who had received communion in the morning were presented with holy cards that contained a prayer for cancer patients. Kraig's name was written on each card, and during the ceremony, our pastor, who celebrated the Mass, called all the children around the altar to recite the prayer for Kraig. It was a lovely thing to do, and I asked Father Gray to express our gratitude to the pastor.

We gathered in the living room on couches and chairs around the coffee table, which was draped with a small linen cloth and adorned with a crucifix, a candle, and Father Gray's chalice in readiness for Mass. It was a sacred and, at the same time, joyous occasion. As we made our petitions, I silently thanked God that Kraig was able to receive his First Communion on earth with his family. Actually, he received two sacraments that day: during the Mass, Father Gray also administered the Sacrament of the Sick and anointed Kraig with the chrism oil. We capped off this beautiful day by celebrating with a big family dinner at a nearby restaurant.

On the day of Kraig's final radiation treatment, as we were driving to the hospital, Mike called us on the car phone with a wonderful surprise. He was making plans for Kraig and me to go to Florida for some fun. Giving Kraig something to look forward to, a gift that would make him happy, typified Mike's perfect planning. It made it possible for Kraig to face that last awful treatment without anxiety.

Mike was not able to leave his job at that time, so he asked our son Brian to go along with us to Florida. It was great fun for Kraig to have his big brother as a companion. Bri took him swimming as often as possible, and they even managed to get in some fishing. Before we left home, Kraig's teacher had given him an assignment, which he took very seriously. He was to bring back a seashell for each of his classmates. Every day, he carefully sifted through the sand, searching out the best shells he could find. They had to be flawless to make the grade. In the beginning, the three of us walked the beach together, but as the days wore on, it became too difficult for Kraig. The afternoon heat was also very hard on him, so we filled some of the time with indoor activities. In the evening, when we went out to eat, we always let Kraig choose the restaurant. The whole idea was to make the vacation as much fun for him as we possibly could.

Before breakfast, I took some time for prayer and meditation by strolling alone on the beach. One day, while sitting on the sand looking out to sea, I caught sight of a couple walking toward me. While still at a distance, one of them commented that the waves were rough and it might not be a good day for swimming. I nodded my head in agreement. To my surprise, the woman said,

"I see you're praying to Padre Pio."

It struck me that it was impossible for her to see the prayer card in my lap from where she stood. As they got close to the spot where I sat, I looked up and smiled.

"You're right, I am praying to Padre Pio," I said. "I am praying for a miracle for my little boy who is eight years old and battling a brain stem tumor." Confiding to strangers was totally out of character for me, but I felt compelled to share my burden. I remember just exploding with:

"I want you to pray for this miracle, too!"

After catching his wife's eye, the man then turned to me with great enthusiasm and said,

"We believe that miracles do happen. My wife has a friend who was miraculously cured."

We chatted for a while, and before they continued their walk, the couple promised to pray for Kraig.

A short time later, another woman approached me.

"Oh, I see you're praying . . . I didn't mean to disturb you," she said.

"You're not disturbing me," I assured her. "I'm praying for something very special."

The next thing I knew, I was telling her all about Kraig, too. Suddenly, a look of wonder came over her.

"I never walk this beach," she said, "but today, for some reason, I had to come here. Now I know why. Nothing touches me more deeply than a mother suffering. You see, I lost my little girl."

"I'm so sorry," I said. My heart went out to this woman who knew what I was feeling.

"I have a sister who is a nun," she continued. "I am going to call her and I guarantee you that all the nuns in her convent will join in the effort to pray for Kraig. As for me, you can be sure that I will pray for him without ceasing."

It was easy to recognize God's presence through these compassionate people who lovingly entered into the widening circle of prayers for Kraig. I prayed that, by word-of-mouth, the network of intercessors would continue to increase. As I was gathering my belongings to head back to the condo, I looked down at my feet and spotted a tiny, perfectly shaped Sand Dollar.[3] This really surprised me because it was not the season when one would normally find such a shell. Perhaps I was reading too much into it, but I have always been charmed by the legend of the Sand Dollar. To have discovered it immediately following my reflection about intercessors struck me as no mere coincidence. I accepted this gift from the sea as a reminder that my plea for a powerful army of intercessors had been heard and was being fulfilled.

Despite a few problems, Florida proved to be a wonderful getaway for Kraig. He was able to

---

3 The Sand Dollar, or the Holy Ghost Shell, is one of the most unusual specimens of marine life. The markings on the shell symbolize the Birth, Crucifixion, and Resurrection of Christ. On the top side of the shell, an outline of the Easter Lily is evident. At the center of the lily appears a five-pointed star representing the Star of Bethlehem. The five narrow openings are representative of the four nail holes and the spear wound made in the body of Christ during the crucifixion. Reversing the shell, you will easily recognize the outline of the Christmas Poinsettia and a bell. When broken, the shell releases five little "birds" called the Doves of Peace. Some say they are the angels that sang to the shepherds the First Christmas Morning.

escape into a world away from doctors, chemo, radiation and all the distress they entail. Bri had to leave two days ahead of us. Knowing what we had to face upon our return, I was in no hurry to get home, but our trip ended on a happy note. The day of departure, Kraig and I arrived at the airport and found it so crowded, we had to wait in line. We finally got our boarding passes, but it wasn't until we neared the gate that I discovered, to my dismay, that we were assigned to separate rows. The flight had obviously been overbooked because other people were experiencing the same problem. I quickly walked up to an airline agent and explained why Kraig could not be alone. He told me to wait for a minute. The next thing I knew, he was handing me two First Class tickets! Yet another unexpected act of kindness that overwhelmed me with gratitude. We were ushered onto the plane ahead of the other passengers, and when the agent came on board he said to the pilot,

"I know you'll want to help this little boy to get back home."

With that, the captain, smiling, looked at me and said, "Mom, you might want to get a picture of this."

Taking Kraig by the hand, he led him to the cockpit. He took his captain's hat off and put it on Kraig's head; then he placed Kraig in the captain's seat while I scrambled to take a picture. It was a thrilling adventure for Kraig, and the picture I took became one of his favorite treasures. All the crew members, without exception, went out of their way to see to Kraig's every need. One stewardess, Beth, spent every free minute she had with us. And it did not end there. A few weeks after we got home, a package, postmarked New Hampshire, arrived in the mail. It was a moose shirt, a gift for Kraig, from Beth and her children.

There are so many good people in this world, and everyone who touched our lives during this time will remain in my heart forever. Through Kraig, I was learning how wide and how deep are the ties of faith and love that bind people. No one can explain fully the mystery of human suffering, but I have learned from firsthand experience that suffering opens hearts to one another.

Chapter VI

A Time to Lose (Eccles. 3:6)

Active involvement in sports had become impossible for Kraig, but he still enjoyed being a spectator, especially at Karl's baseball games where he was the Mustangs' greatest fan. Karl's friend, Matt, who had always doted on Kraig, was one of the best players on the team, and the one who hit the most home runs. At one of the games, Kraig turned to me and said,

"Matt told me he was going to hit a home run for me tonight."

Matt's mother, seated nearby, couldn't help but overhear. Worried, for fear Kraig might be disappointed, she turned around and said,

"I don't know, Kraig . . . sometimes Matt hits home runs and sometimes he strikes out."

Kraig acknowledged her remark but shook his head with self-assurance.

"No," he said, "Matt told me he is going to hit a home run for me."

When Matt got up to the plate, his mother and I

shared an anxious moment, but then, "pow!" Matt slammed that ball right out of the park. Kraig was wild with excitement as I helped him down from the bleachers and over to the fence where Matt was waiting to give him the "high five." It was a great thrill for all of us.

The Mustangs were slated to go on to the finals, and Kraig wanted to do something extra special for Matt to show his support. From the time he could hold a pencil, Kraig had shown a lot of artistic promise, but since the tumor, his ability to draw was severely hampered. Nevertheless, he worked as hard as he could to complete a picture on which he inscribed the words "Matt The Home Run Champion."

The Mustangs proved their mettle by going on to win the championship. On that day, the fans hooted and hollered with enthusiasm as they watched all the team members receive their special championship T-shirts. Then the coach called Kraig down from the stands and said,

"I would like to present this T-shirt to Kraig Frick, our biggest fan."

Everyone stood up and applauded as the coach held the shirt up to Kraig's chest for all to see. With a lump in my throat, I clapped my hands for Kraig, the biggest champion of all, who had endured the glare of the hot Texas sun while cheering the team to their ultimate triumph. It was quite a day for Matt who, amid many well deserved accolades, received the coveted game baseball, but I think Kraig's drawing meant more to him than all the glory that goes with victory.

* * *

Praying for a miracle cure was steadily drawing me deeper into my Catholic faith. I had always loved and practiced my religion, and turned to God often in prayer, but Kraig's situation had given an added intensity to my spiritual life. As I sought the aid of friends on earth and in heaven, I found my heart widening to embrace a deeper realization of the term "Communion of Saints." It became very important to me to learn all that I could about the saints and holy ones I was asking to intercede on Kraig's behalf. I discovered, for example, that neither Marie of the Incarnation nor Padre Pio[4] had been officially declared saints in the Catholic Church. The process of canonization (formal sainthood) takes years, and one of the criteria necessary is proof of bona fide miracles through the candidate's intercession. I wanted Kraig to be one of those miracles.

I needed to "do my homework," so to speak, so I drove over to Sacred Heart Catholic Bookstore one morning to see what I could find. I asked the woman behind the counter if there was anything available on Padre Pio's life. With a warm smile on her face, she circled around to one of the many bookstands.

---

4 In 2002, Padre Pio was officially declared a Saint.

"Padre Pio is a particular favorite of mine. I would highly recommend this book," she said, pointing to a biography by Bernard Ruffin.[5]

I picked it up, leafed through several pages, then looked at her and said,

"We are praying for a miracle cure . . ."

Before I could finish, she asked,

"Are you Mrs. Frick?"

Somewhat surprised, I answered,

"Yes, I am."

She offered me her hand and said,

"I am so pleased to meet you. My name is Janet and I have been praying for your son."

I was astounded. Then I discovered that not only Janet, but every employee at Sacred Heart Bookstore was praying for Kraig as well. As it turned out, Janet was a member of my parish. She had been present one day in the chapel when prayers were requested for Kraig and had followed through by spreading the word to her colleagues at Sacred Heart. Given the size of All Saints Parish and the number of services each Sunday, it wasn't unusual that we had never met before. After chatting a bit and realizing how important Padre Pio was to me, she gently touched my arm and asked,

5 Ruffin, Bernard C., Padre Pio: The True Story (Huntington: Our Sunday Visitor, 1982).

"Do you have a few minutes to spare?"

"Yes," I answered.

"I have something for you, but it's at home. I live very close to the store and I can have it here in ten minutes."

I browsed through the aisles of the bookstore while I waited, wondering what it was Janet wanted to give me. She returned with a beautifully handcarved, wooden plaque of Padre Pio. A regular customer who knew of her deep affection for Padre Pio had carved it and given it to her just days before. With tears in her eyes, she placed it into my hands.

"I know this is meant for you, and it would give me great joy if you would accept it along with my prayers."

I was speechless! Once again, God had blessed me through a perfect stranger. When I got home, I placed the plaque next to Kraig's bed, which Mike and I had moved into our room.

This would not be the only sign of intercession to find a place near Kraig. On the day of his First Holy Communion, we had given him a medal of St. James, his patron saint, which he constantly wore around his neck. Other medals arrived from all over the world. The most dramatic of these deliveries came through a network of prayer that began with an Ignatian retreat I had made a few years back. When it was over, the group continued to meet on a regular basis. Naturally, with Kraig so ill, I couldn't attend the monthly meetings, but my friends in the group continued to keep me in their prayers. One day, a guest from the Missionaries of Charity came to speak to the group. After my friends sought her prayers for Kraig, she contacted Mother Teresa in Calcutta. Mother Teresa personally sent us three Miraculous Medals, one for Kraig, one for Mike, and one for me. She also sent her picture with a personal note reading,

"Dear Kraig, Jesus loves you very much. You are precious to Him. God bless you."

We were so thrilled when those medals arrived at our door!

It was impossible to wear all of the medals that we received, so I began pinning them to Kraig's pillow. The Padre Pio woodcarving fit in beautifully with these other reminders that prayer was pouring in from all sides for Kraig.

* * *

With the radiation treatments behind him, Kraig now had to undergo chemotherapy. I decided that, for every trip to the hospital, he could choose a fun thing to do. Kraig did not have a great deal of wants. His demands were small. On the way home from a treatment, if his stomach was okay, he might ask to stop for a Slurpee or a cherry-limeade ~ simple things ~ yet, it was something to look forward to, and that was important.

Mike stayed as present as possible to us during this time. When things slowed down at work, he would go in late to the office so that he could devote the extra time to Kraig. Since chemotherapy would sometimes keep Kraig and me at the hospital all day, we had to come up with a lunch plan. There was a bagel shop nearby and Kraig just loved their sandwiches. On chemo mornings, before Kraig and I left for the hospital, Mike would run out and pick up some bagel sandwiches for us. No matter what the demands might have been at work, Mike let us know in one way or the other that he was always with us.

Kraig and I spent a lot of time together driving back and forth for treatments. Very often, when he was alone in the back of the car, he would reveal his deepest feelings. After my accident, I remember once telling him that he was my hero. He must have mulled this over in his mind for a long time. On one of our trips coming home from chemo, the song "The Wind Beneath My Wings" was playing on the radio. When it came to the part, "Did you ever know that you're my hero?" I began to sing the words to Kraig. He let me finish before saying,

"Mom, you always said grandpop was your hero."

"Yes, honey, it's true. grandpop is my hero, but you were the one who ran back to the cabin to get help the day I fell off the mountain, and because of you, I was rescued. In everything you've ever done, and most especially now, your courage and strength comes through and you will always be a hero to me."

I can still see him smiling from ear to ear, so proud. From that day on, I claimed "The Wind Beneath My Wings" as my own personal tribute to Kraig, and it will forever remain our song.

In June, midway through the chemo, a social worker from the hospital approached us with an offer from the *Make A Wish Foundation*, an organization that does their best to fulfill a terminally ill child's dream. Realizing the nature of the foundation's work, and what this meant for our family, made the meeting particularly hard on us, even more so because the offer was presented in the presence of Kraig. While acknowledging that the *Make a Wish Foundation* performs a wonderful service for many, I knew that Kraig didn't need anything spectacular in his life. He was truly happiest when he was with the family. Mike and I were not sure how to respond to the social worker, but Kraig himself broke the silence by letting his wishes be known.

"What I really want to do is to go back to Colorado," he announced.

The doctor, who happened to be in the room with us, looked over at him and smiled.

"Well, then, let's arrange it! We have a chemotherapy schedule we have to follow, but I will call the hospital in Denver and request a doctor there to continue the series. It will mean two or three trips into Denver."

Kraig was beaming, and in the spirit of the moment, I added a few promises to make his joy complete.

"I'll tell you what, honey. Before we drive into Denver for the first treatment, we'll go to your favorite candy store and buy a box of taffy just for you, and you can eat as much as you want."

Kraig loved that idea.

"And another thing," I continued, "Why don't we get a new moose while we are in Colorado? Then you can take your new moose to Denver with you."

With all the details having been worked out with the hospital in Denver, we left for the cabin in early July. While the trip may have been primarily for Kraig, finding refuge in the rugged Rocky Mountains was a wonderful tonic for all of us. To be surrounded by such beauty on all sides is like nestling in the embrace of God. So far removed from everyday stress, one cannot help but feel a measure of peace and serenity.

Despite the necessary trips into Denver, we wanted Kraig to experience a normal, family vacation atmosphere at the cabin. Klaire brought along a few friends, and Mike's sister Maggie and her son joined us, too. With Karl and Dan, we had a full house. Kraig's participation in physical activities was rather limited, but he enjoyed the companionship of the kids and joined in the video and board games. It was heartbreaking, though, to observe him watching the other kids head out the back door to hike and climb. Kraig, who had thrived on outdoor activity, could not even climb the stairs. In fact, when he went to bed at night, Mike had to carry him to the bathroom because he was not able to navigate the few steps from the bedroom to the landing where the bathroom is located.

Before our first trip to the hospital in Denver, I drove into town one day and found a new moose. Kraig named it "Scratchy," but later changed the name to "Sparkey." In the end, the newest member of the moose family became known as "Scratchy-Sparkey."

On the day of our first chemo appointment, Karl and Dan came along. We had to spend the better part of the day at the hospital, so Kraig was happy to have his family with him. During the drive, he sat quietly in the back of the car with the box of taffy on his lap and Scratchy-Sparkey serving as a cushion. Going to a new facility with unfamiliar people was very frightening for Kraig, but the doctor and nurses could not have been kinder. The atmosphere was so pleasant, in fact, that it eased the way for return trips.

One early evening, heading back for the

mountains, we were driving through Denver when Kraig shouted from the back of the car,

"Look, a moose!"

"What are you talking about, Kraig? I don't see a moose," I said.

"Back there," he pointed.

He had seen the back of a billboard with a moose cutout. When we turned the car around to get a look at the front, we discovered it was an ad for Moosehead Beer. To Kraig's delight, Mike promised to buy a six-pack just so he could add the empty bottles to his moose memorabilia collection.

Then came the Sunday morning, so precious in my memory, that heaven had arranged for our consolation. All the kids except Dan and Kraig were going water rafting, and I had volunteered to drive them into Estes Park where they would meet up with the tour bus. I had to pass St. Malo's on the way back to the cabin. *Hope springs eternal*, as they say, and riding alone in the car, I found myself pleading once again with God for a miracle. The closer I got to St. Malo's Chapel, the more I felt drawn to make a visit. I let myself be drawn. When I opened the door and saw that a Mass was in progress and several men were kneeling in prayer, I hesitated for a moment, but the need to be there surpassed all awkwardness. I slid into the last pew in the back of the church with every intention of remaining quiet and inconspicuous. A few moments later, I found myself asking for prayers for my son.

I have thought about that day on numerous occasions and still marvel at the perfection of God's timing. Here we were, Jacques and I, two people, who just happened to be in a remote area of Colorado at the same time, both carrying the same cross for our loved ones. That alone would have been enough to launch a friendship. But, God had been working behind the scenes setting up circumstances that would create an even deeper affinity between us. Our friendship, right from the start, was to be part of a spiritual network. As Jacques discovered my correspondence with Sister Noel, and my prayers to Marie of the Incarnation, before whose tomb he had proclaimed "Yes" to his vocation, his generous heart felt "at home" with us. His instant rapport with Kraig was the proof of a bond already fashioned by Divine intervention. Actually, everyone in the family who met Jacques felt at ease with him, as with an old friend. I simply cannot find an *earthly* explanation for the depth of our feelings.

Scripture talks about an appointed time for all things. I am convinced that Jacques' entrance into our lives was in God's appointed time, to help lift up our hearts. Our meeting with Jacques seemed like a confirmation that we were not alone. Our hopes for a miracle soared. Jacques, too, felt that Divine Providence was acting with purpose on behalf of all of us. A week after our first meeting, Mike and I received this letter confirming the bond that we had felt between us:

July 28, 1996

Dear Karyl & Mike,

Kraig and your whole family have been so much a part of my thoughts and prayers since we first met that providential Sunday, on the 21st of July. That same afternoon, I went for a long walk to a beautiful waterfall deep in the woods in back of the St. Malo Retreat Center. My prayers, at the foot of that waterfall, were for both my father and Kraig. Before leaving that sacred piece of ground, I picked two rocks, a red flat one for Kraig, and a grey granite rock for my father. These two rocks now lay on top of my breviary and have become a daily reminder of placing my prayer intentions for my father and Kraig at the foot of our true Rock and Savior Jesus Christ. When I pray the "Our Father," I find it easier for me to say (in respect to my father and Kraig): "May your dream for my father and your dream for Kraig be done." I may not know what God's dream is for either of them, but one thing I do know: Because of my faith, I truly trust God's dream for each one of us, and that just might include a miracle or two! Let us remain in union of prayer for that special blessing, whatever it may be. And through our prayers of hope, of trust, of expectations, of compassion, of confidence, of reliance, of solicitude, and of optimism, let us never forget the RESURRECTION! Also, please be assured that the prayers of our whole Franciscan community here at St. Malo's continue to be with all of you.

I hope that your trip back home was safe and uneventful. The news back home is that my father is doing well at the moment and planning to attend my solemn profession in September. I continue to pray that he will be able to be there and that he will continue to remain healthy during the whole of his stay away from his home.

Today, it is pouring rain here in Allenspark. I will be writing letters to special spiritual friends of mine, requesting their prayers for both my father and Kraig. Yesterday, I went back to the Mountain Meadow Cafe with a friar. We had another great breakfast. I had the pancakes this time (the smaller, two portion.) You were very much in my mind and in my heart during the whole of this meal.

Do give my best friendship wishes to Kraig, to Dan and to the rest of the family. Take care and may God's blessings be upon you all. And, trust me, I'm still in heavy deliberations with Mother Mary of the Incarnation and Padre Pio.

Your Franciscan friend and brother in Christ,

Jacques

Mike and I savored every word of Jacques' letter and shared it with the children. We could feel the strength of his prayers and thanked God for placing him in our lives.

Soon after our meeting with Jacques, Kraig's tumor began to manifest new and troubling symptoms that required even more spiritual vigilance in order to preserve our peace of heart. Drastic changes erupted in Kraig's behavior. Under normal conditions, these acts of uncontrolled temper would have greatly disturbed me, but by the grace of God, I understood that this was not my son at work, but the mean, ugly tumor that was swelling inside of him. It nearly tore my heart out to see how successfully it had invaded the beautiful brain of my child and bent his sweet disposition to do its bidding.

Perhaps the most dramatic example of Kraig's personality change had to do with the aquarium that Luke had given him. One day, without warning, the *tumor* hit that aquarium and shattered it into a million pieces. Fish were all over the floor. We picked them up as quickly as we could, but only one tiny fish survived. We named this gritty little goldfish "Ish" and placed it in a small glass bowl on the kitchen counter. The shattered aquarium was terribly upsetting, but I would not allow it to shatter my hope for a miracle. Ish became a symbol of life for me. If this lone little goldfish could survive such a calamity, then maybe it was a sign that Kraig would also survive.

Chapter VII

A Time to Heal (Eccles. 3:3)

While we were still in Colorado, we received a letter from the locutionist. She wanted us to know that she had received a message for us from the Blessed Mother:

"Kraig is suffering so that one might be saved."

These words really bothered Mike because he felt that it meant Kraig was going to die. I did not interpret it that way at all. I tried to reassure Mike with the second part of the message:

"Kraig is being held in the arms of the Blessed Mother."

After making the prayer pact with Jacques, my confidence in the power of intercession was bolstered and I went about expanding my outreach. I sent a letter off to the National Center of Padre Pio seeking prayers for Kraig and Fernand, Jacques' father. Meanwhile, Jacques contacted the Ursuline nuns in Canada with the same request. I also circulated copies of my prayers to Marie of the Incarnation and Padre Pio to the rosary group at

Mary Immaculate School, asking them to include Fernand in their daily rosary for Kraig.

Kraig was growing weaker with each passing day. Here was my child, who had had the courage and tenacity to save me after my fall. Now, more than life itself, I wanted to save him. For a long time, I was haunted with the thought: *Why didn't I die on that mountain? I could be in heaven right now helping Kraig!* With the passage of time, however, I came to realize that Kraig had to save me so that I could be there to care for him. He needed my physical presence, and I needed this special time with him. Kraig was not the huggy-lovey kind, but during the time I cared for him, he showered me with more hugs and kisses than in all his growing up years put together. On one particularly difficult day, I kissed his cheek and exclaimed,

"Kraig, you're the greatest!"

Instead of smiling with self-satisfaction, as he did usually, he looked up at me and said,

"No, Mom, you're the greatest!"

Kraig's story wasn't unfolding in a vacuum. There were other family members whose needs had to be met. But I must say that all our children displayed an understanding and generosity over and above anything I could have imagined. Each one of them made an effort to spend time with Kraig. Mike and I were very proud to see the way everyone pulled together. As in happy times, we were all in this together.

After Jacques left the retreat at St. Malo's, he headed for Washington, D.C. where he lived in a house with other Franciscans while continuing his studies for the priesthood.

The date for his solemn vows had been set for September 7th in Hartford, Connecticut. Despite his heavy schedule, Jacques remained steadfast in his solicitude for Kraig, as we did for Fernand. Meanwhile, in Canada, his mother watched helplessly as the cancerous tumor continued unabated in her husband's brain. Fernand had opted to forego chemotherapy and radiation, so there was virtually nothing anyone could do but pray. To complicate matters, shortly after refusing therapy, Fernand had suffered a heart attack. Jacques was beginning to accept the fact that his father would probably not be around for his ordination.

I felt a tremendous bond with Mrs. LaPointe. She and her husband were French-speaking Canadians and, while they both understood English, neither of them was comfortable communicating in a second language. Jacques was the go-between for us. He conveyed to them my empathy with their suffering and my communion in prayer and hope. Jacques assured his parents that Fernand was connected to Kraig in a vast network of prayer which through our combined efforts (Jacques' and mine) had literally criss-crossed continents. It was humbling, indeed, to realize that we were but a small link in a mighty chain being forged by the Holy Spirit.

Fernand's condition went from bad to worse. While recovering from the heart attack, he suffered a stroke. Not wanting to prolong his agony, the doctor asked Jacques' mother for permission not to resuscitate if Fernand sustained yet another heart attack. Before agreeing to dismiss treatment, she wanted to know how far the cancer had progressed. It was mutually agreed that as soon as Fernand regained his strength, an MRI would be taken to determine the status of the tumor. I felt so bad for Jacques. His father was so gravely ill, it would be impossible for him to travel the necessary distance to watch Jacques receive his solemn vows.

In Dallas, the battle against Kraig's tumor raged on until the doctors informed us that nothing more could be done. From then on, all we could hope for was to keep Kraig as comfortable as possible. Mike and I had been hoping to wean Kraig away from the steroids, but his doctor advised against it. He also suggested getting assistance from the Hospice organization, so that Kraig could receive his continuing medical care at home. We wanted to do all of Kraig's primary care ourselves, but we did take advantage of a Hospice social worker and a nurse from St. Paul's Hospital.

Summer was drawing to a close, and I still had to shop for school supplies and uniforms. Early one morning, after I had just put together a list of what the kids needed, the phone rang. To my surprise, it was Jacques. Right away, I sensed tentativeness in his voice.

"Karyl, I have some unbelievable news for you and Mike."

Thinking for one split second that he might have experienced some hint of Divine intervention for Kraig, I tried to catch my breath and asked,

"What is it, Jacques?"

I could feel my heart racing in anticipation as he began to speak.

"Our prayers for a miracle cure for my father have been answered. God has blessed him with a complete healing ~ the tumor is gone!"

I tried to grasp what he had just said. It was such a stunning surprise. Jacques continued to pour out the details, including the fact that the paralysis his father sustained as a result of the stroke had also disappeared.

"After the stroke, my mother was bracing herself for my father's death. For some reason, she insisted on having further tests to check the tumor's progress. When my father was physically able, he went back to the hospital. After the scans were completed and the radiologist had looked at them, he personally apologized to my father, explaining that the machine was not working properly and they would have to repeat the procedure. Karyl, there was absolutely nothing wrong with their machine. A second set of pictures, identical to the first, finally convinced the doctor that the tumor had disappeared!"

I could not fight the tears, but they were tears of joy.

"Oh, Jacques, I am so happy for you and your family. Our prayers have been answered!"

There was a pause. The tone of Jacques' voice had changed. He knew full well how gravely ill Kraig was, and his sensitivity to our circumstances made it difficult for him to rejoice. I did not want to spoil his personal miracle ~ I wanted him to know that we shared in his joy. I repeatedly lauded God's mercy and our gratitude for answered prayer, but I could sense there was something else bothering him. As the conversation unfolded, I discovered that he was deeply troubled about a dream he had had about Kraig. In the dream, Kraig had appeared to be quite concerned. Looking right into Jacques' eyes, he had asked Jacques in a very serious tone:

"Will you be with my family at all the important times of their life?"

"Yes, Kraig, I promise you I will," had been Jacques' answer.

The dream had had such a strong effect on Jacques that he hesitated to tell me about it, yet he felt it was almost a betrayal of Kraig to keep silent. As painful as it was to hear, I was grateful he shared it with me. The ramifications of the dream were not yet mine to know, but like the Mother of Our Lord and Savior, I pondered this event with the many other signs and wonders stored in my heart.

On September 4th, Meg came to Dallas. She wanted to spend Kraig's birthday with him and made arrangements to stay at another friend's house. The day she arrived, we feared whether or not Kraig would make it to his birthday. A few weeks earlier, when Meg had spoken to him on the phone, she had said,

"You know Kraig, this is your *golden birthday* because you will be nine years old on the ninth of September. That means you can have anything you want from your godmother."

Kraig had wanted to think about it for a while. A few days later, he asked me to call Meg back. With as much enthusiasm as he could muster, he said,

"I want a lizard ~ a green lizard."

"One green lizard coming up!" Meg responded.

From the time he was able to speak, Kraig never called Meg anything but Godmother Meg. They had a unique relationship based not only on love, but also on a genuine mutual admiration for each other.

Shortly after that phone call, Kraig became dreadfully ill. Meg still wanted to come but, under the circumstances, she did not bring a present. The tumor was at its ugliest, and Meg had never seen Kraig in such a state. The following day, there was a marked improvement. Meg came back to the house to visit. As we were standing around Kraig's bed, he suddenly announced that he wanted everyone out of the room except Godmother Meg. Obviously perplexed, Meg looked at us, raising her eyebrows, as we quietly left the room. He then told her to shut the door. The rest of us stood right outside and couldn't help but overhear Kraig say,

"They all think I'm mean. Do you think I'm mean?"

"No, Kraig, I don't think you're mean," Meg said.

He repeated again, "They think I'm mean."

With that, Meg asked,

"What do you want me to do?"

"I want you to go out there and tell them I am not mean and that I have never been mean."

Meg opened the door and was surprised to observe the bunch of us, all huddled together and crouched down in the hall out of Kraig's line of sight. Trying desperately not to laugh, she feigned a stern expression, and shouted,

"I want everyone to know that Kraig is not

mean!"

We were smiling at the absurdity of the situation while, at the same time, wiping away our tears. Once again, Kraig called out from his room,

"Godmother Meg, come here! You tell them if they say anything about me being mean, you will kick them out of the house."

Meg dutifully came out with the latest pronouncement and when she returned to Kraig's side, he smiled at her and said,

"That was pretty good!"

Kraig had no more control over the tumor than we did, yet he worried about how his behavior was affecting the rest of the family. Using Meg as a go-between he was able to tell us how much it mattered to him that we understood.

September 7: the day stands out in my memory like the sound of a bell in the night. Far away in Hartford, Connecticut, Jacques LaPointe was to make his solemn vows as a Franciscan. For us in Dallas, the day meant bearing witness to Kraig's worst suffering yet.

Our son, Bri, had every intention of driving from Boston to Hartford to represent the family at Jacques' ceremony, but in light of Kraig's sudden turn for the worse, he had come back to Dallas immediately. But we did not forget Jacques. I spoke to him early in the morning on September 7 and assured him that even though none of us could be there in person, we would all be united in prayer as he pledged his entire life to God. He promised to call later in the afternoon.

This day was unquestionably the day when Kraig was the sickest he had ever been. He was in and out of consciousness. As the hours wore on, there was so much confusion with all that was happening, I didn't even notice that the Hospice people were still around. Debbie, the Hospice social worker, told me later that she had not expected Kraig to make it through the day.

Sometime during the late morning, I sat down on Kraig's bed, placing myself behind him as a sort of backrest. It was easier for him to breathe in an upright position. Mike, Meg, and all of our children were surrounding the bed and, together, we joined in prayer. Suddenly, Kraig spoke up, loud and clear. To our surprise, he called out::

"Jacques."

Kraig had not uttered a word in two days; then this ~ and nothing more! We were baffled. What could possibly have drawn his thoughts to Jacques enough for him to pronounce his name so clearly? Then, a thought flashed through my mind. I slowly looked around the room at everyone and said,

"I wonder if Jacques is receiving communion at this very moment."

I didn't think anything more about it. The

lunch hour had arrived, and, one by one, the kids went to the kitchen to grab a bite to eat. Meg, Bri and I stayed in the room with Kraig. After propping him up on some pillows, I bent over and tenderly caressing his cheek, I said,

"Oh, Kraig, I love you."

With great difficulty, he slowly opened his eyes and spoke:

"I . . .love . . .you . . .too."

"Did you hear that, Mom?" Bri cried out.

Meg was too dumbfounded to speak. It was unbelievable. Smiling through tears, I looked at both of them and then whispered a prayer of thanksgiving. There have been other times in my life when I heard these same words from my children, but this was different. It was almost physically impossible for Kraig to speak; yet, he managed to give me this priceless gift, a gift I will cherish for as long as I live.

Shortly after that, Kraig fell back into a deep sleep. It was then that Jacques called. I took the portable phone out into the hall, just outside of Kraig's room, so I could keep an eye on him while talking.

"Oh, Jacques, I'm so glad you called. The strangest thing happened this morning while we were praying in Kraig's room. All of a sudden, he called out your name. Kraig hasn't spoken in two days!"

There was a long silence, followed by Jacques' question:

"Karyl, do you remember what time it was when this happened?"

As to the precise moment, it wasn't just my word, but Mike got on the other phone and both of us told him exactly what the time was when Kraig spoke. Jacques was astounded.

"Karyl, I cannot begin to describe to you how strongly I felt Kraig's presence with me today. When we spoke this morning, I worried for fear something would happen to him while I was making my vows. It never crossed my mind that something would happen to me!"

"What do you mean, Jacques'?"

"It was during the Mass. You know how there is a small, thin line in the form of a cross on every Eucharistic host?"

"Yes," I replied.

"Well, the line is so thin, it is impossible to see it from a distance, but during Mass, as my provincial elevated the host, I fixed my eyes on it. I could see the cross come out from the host in a very marked way. Without having to think, I was blessed with an instant inner knowledge that it was Christ's cross. Then, I saw Kraig carrying that cross. He seemed to be carrying the cross of Christ for himself and for my father. It wasn't a spiritual fantasy. I knew that, in some mysterious way, Kraig was with me."

I responded tearfully,

"I don't think I ever told you this Jacques, but a woman, a locutionist who has been praying for Kraig, made a statement that fits exactly with what you've just told me. Her actual words were: Kraig is suffering so that one might be saved."

"Karyl, that one has to be my father ~ and perhaps others as well. And that's not all ~ it was at the very moment Kraig called out my name in Dallas that I saw him in the host!"

By now, tears were streaming down my cheeks. I looked down at Kraig, sleeping like an angel. With my voice cracking, I struggled to say,

"You know, Jacques, I had really hoped if Kraig had been healed that God would call him to be a priest, because I thought he would be able to use the experience of his illness to minister to others."

In almost a whisper, Jacques said,

"Don't you give it another thought, Karyl, because Kraig is already a part of my ministry."

Kraig's suffering grew more intense as night fell. Mike and I took turns holding him up as he desperately battled to breathe. The rest of the family was sort of scattered all around the house, each one trying to snatch a little sleep. In the wee hours of the morning, the labored breathing subsided and Kraig fell into a peaceful slumber.

When he awakened, to our amazement, he asked for something to eat. Kraig had not left his room in days and had not eaten a bite of food during that time. We put him in the wheelchair and took him to the kitchen where he eagerly polished off two bowls of cereal. Then he said he wanted to be with the others in the living room. We all sat around shaking our heads in disbelief as he joined in the conversation. He was completely coherent, talking to all of us. Karl was sitting in a chair with a photo album in his lap. He walked over to show Kraig some old family pictures. The two of them poured over the album together, giggling while they shared one story after another about the past. None of us could believe what we were seeing. Just hours before, this precious child was hovering between life and death. In fact, we had even sent for Father Gray. Now, we all sat transfixed, observing this dramatic and unbelievable change.

In addition to being the day before Kraig's birthday, September 8 also happens to be the day the Church celebrates the birthday of the Blessed Mother. Didn't the locutionist tell us that Mary was holding Kraig in her arms? I kept my counsel, yet I could not help but secretly wonder if Kraig's remarkable improvement was merely a prelude to my miracle. God had healed Fernand when things looked darkest. Maybe He was doing the same for Kraig.

Euphoria swept through the house when Kraig happily announced that he wanted to celebrate his birthday with a party. I quickly called Meg who, with no gift ready, made immediate plans to go shopping with Kraig's brothers and sisters. They searched all over Dallas until they found a green lizard. All of the kids got caught up in the excitement and scrambled to find just the right present. Mike and I already had a gift for Kraig: two containers of metallic baseball cards. They just had to be wrapped. Also, when we were in Colorado, I had found a watch, trimmed in wood, with the face of a moose on the dial. I had bought it and tucked it away for Kraig's big day. I had also baked a moose cake and stored it in the freezer. All we needed was some ice cream and maybe a few balloons and streamers. This birthday was going to be a celebration like none we had ever had!

Suddenly, Kraig announced that he wanted to go look for baseball cards! He also wanted a *glow-in-the-dark* Halloween mask. So, that afternoon, Luke and Meg took him for a ride in Luke's Suburban. Meg was convinced Kraig knew he would not be around for Halloween and that was why he was so insistent about the mask. She ran into one of Dallas's huge supermarkets and approached a clerk who was busily stocking shelves. He apologized, explaining that the

Halloween things were not on display yet.

"I don't care," Meg persisted. "I need a mask and I need it today!" Believe it or not, the clerk found one in the back and it *did* glow in the dark. Kraig was so excited when Meg got back to the car and presented the mask to him.

"Can you come back to Dallas on Halloween?" he pleaded. "We could *Trick or Treat* together. You could bring your kids, too. It would be so much fun."

Trying not to break down, Meg promised to try to arrange something; then she hugged Kraig and told him how much she loved him.

The following morning, we all got up early and gathered together to watch Kraig open his presents. It was Mike's birthday, too, but everyone's attention, especially Mike's, was riveted on Kraig. Bri's present was a special pack of baseball cards. When you buy the pack, there is no way of knowing the value of the individual cards inside because the pack is sealed. A wonderful surprise for Kraig was finding a Frank Thomas baseball card worth $40.00. He thought that was so cool! He made a fuss over every gift and was especially pleased with the green lizard. We sang "Happy Birthday" and watched with delight as Kraig attempted to blow out the candles. With a little unseen help, he got his wish. All in all, it was a glorious day, one I will be eternally grateful for because, to everyone's dismay, by evening, Kraig started to go downhill again.

After such a magnificent high, we all had to emotionally switch gears. The rapid reversal of Kraig's rally was a heart-wrenching experience that defied description. When someone you love is suffering, each minute seems to drag on forever. Every day, the effects of the tumor became more devastating. Sometimes, without warning, Kraig would scream outrageous things and I remember once, in anguish, confiding to Jacques:

"Isn't it enough that this vicious tumor is squeezing the life out of Kraig's body? Does it have to distort his personality as well?"

"Karyl, listen to me carefully," Jacques said. "I want you to understand that you are now witnessing a spiritual battle. The devil is making a last desperate effort to hold onto a soul destined for heaven."

Jacques' words made a lot of sense to me. From that time on, when these frightful tirades occurred, I would calmly call out the name of Jesus, and in a matter of minutes, Kraig seemed enveloped in peace.

A few days later, we received the following note from Jacques:

Dear Friends,

You are so much in my thoughts and in my prayers. And when I find myself thinking of Kraig,

I also find myself closer to God. Kraig will indeed always remain an important part of my priesthood, and so will the Frick family as a whole. I truly believe that through your intercession, my father received the grace of a physical healing ~ just as I believe that God has called me to be a part of the spiritual healing in Kraig's illness. We are truly there for each other; brothers and sisters in Christ.

My father is coming out of the hospital today. I also pray that this day will be a day of special graces for Kraig.

All my love goes to you with this letter.
Jacques, OFM

With Fernand returning to his family, and Kraig slipping further and further from us, I experienced the delicate, poignant balance of divine economy. I knew in my heart that the intertwining of our lives, of Jacques' family and ours, had not been by accident. It was like watching a puzzle come together from small, interlocking pieces, each piece building upon another. I could not help but wonder how many more pieces were left.

Chapter VIII

A Time to Die (Eccles. 3:2)

During the daylight hours of September 16, Kraig was on the sofa in the living room, with me seated next to him, my hand on his pulse. His heartbeat and respiration would stop; then, all of a sudden, he would begin gasping for breath again. Each of these episodes lasted a matter of seconds, but served to prolong his agony for hours. By evening, he was more peaceful. Mike carried him to our room and gently put him in our bed. There was no change during the night. Both of us were thankful to God that the morning found Kraig still resting comfortably. He looked almost serene as he lay there sleeping. Sometimes he would stir slightly, but he showed no signs of discomfort. At one point, he opened his eyes and asked for a drink of water, then promptly settled back to sleep.

Early in the afternoon, Mike went to check on things at the office. I lay down on the bed beside Kraig. I was reading the last of three books I had bought on Padre Pio, this one detailing the physical evidence of his stigmata. When I finished, I went over to the mantle and picked up a picture of Kraig that was placed in front of the Padre Pio woodcarving. I had sent this photo to the Padre Pio Foundation, and they had touched it to the blood and gloves of Padre Pio before returning it to me. I placed the picture on Kraig's forehead and then put it back on the woodcarving.

I picked up *The Little Prince*, a book that had been sent to Mike and Kraig for their joint birthday from an old school friend of Mike's. I began reading it aloud to Kraig. I was in chapter nine: the Little Prince is preparing to leave his planet, and the rose confesses her love for him saying, "Well, of course, I love you. It is my fault that you have not known it all the while . . ." Suddenly, Kraig's breathing changed significantly. I recognized the sign and immediately put the book down and called Mike.

"Do you want to be here?"

"Yes," he answered. In the background, the chimes from our clock could be heard striking three times. Mike whispered,

"Karyl, it's the Hour of Divine Mercy!"

At that very instant, I looked down at Kraig and watched our precious child draw his final breath.

"You will not die one moment before nor one moment after God calls you . . ."

I closed my eyes and whispered, "Into Your

Hands, I commend his spirit."

Mike was home within minutes. When he came into our room, he found me on my knees, praying the third decade of the rosary. He quietly knelt down by my side and we finished the rosary together.

I felt in my heart that the Blessed Mother was cradling our son, just as she had her own after his descent from the cross. Understanding the spiritual magnitude of what had just taken place, however, in no way lessened my natural grief. Before and after that moment, my comfort in Jesus and Mary is in knowing that I have never once had to explain to them what it is like to go through such pain. Gripped in sorrow, I laid there holding Kraig in my arms. I just could not let go.

The phone rang. It was Klaire. She just had an awful feeling that something was wrong and, following her instincts, had run out of class to make the call. Mike told her what had happened and offered to pick her up at school, but she insisted she would be able to drive herself home. Mike called Luke who left immediately to come to the house; then he contacted Ginger in Fort Worth and Bri in Boston. When Luke arrived, he called his wife Regina. It was her birthday. Trying to sound casual, he asked her to come over to his parents' house after work. Mike left to pick up Karl and Dan. He wanted to be the one to tell them about Kraig.

While Mike was gone, an attendant from the funeral home came to pick up our son's body, and it was Luke who carried Kraig through the house to the waiting van in the garage. Letting go of my baby was the hardest thing I have ever done in my life. In the grief of the moment, we didn't make the connection, but the following spring, during the Mass for Palm Sunday, Luke was awestruck by the reading on Joseph of Arimethea. In the Catholic Church, before receiving the Sacrament of Confirmation, most teachers encourage their pupils to select a saint's name that has some personal meaning for them, usually a saint they would like to emulate. Luke had chosen Joseph for his Confirmation name ~ not St. Joseph, husband of Mary and foster-father of Jesus, but Joseph of Arimethea. As he sat there in the pew, he was overwhelmed by the profound, seemingly prophetic choice he had made. It was Joseph of Arimethea who had carried Christ's body to the tomb. It struck Luke that maybe it was more than happenstance that he was the one who carried the lifeless body of his baby brother (who also happened to be his godson) to the point where it would be taken to be prepared for burial.

Grief is as individual as one's fingerprints. Mike and I were careful to respect the feelings of each of the children. They could see what was happening, and each of them felt a measure of relief that Kraig's suffering was over, even though to the very end, they held onto the belief that there would be a medical miracle. The finality of death takes a long time to sink in and none of us had come near that plateau yet.

Jacques had been anxiously awaiting some word. When I was able to compose myself, I called to tell him that Kraig had left for heaven. He did not have to articulate his feelings ~ the intimacy of our shared burden spoke volumes. He did talk about what an important day it was for Franciscans: September 17 is the feast of St. Francis of Assisi's stigmata. How strange that in the moments before Kraig's death I had been reading of these holy wounds on the body of Padre Pio. It struck both of us that the day and hour of Kraig's departure was all part of God's design.

There was no question but that Jacques would be coming for the funeral.

"I'll call right now and make reservations," Jacques told me. "Will you please find a hotel located nearby?"

"You will stay here with us ~ on that, we insist. Just let us know the day and time and we will come to pick you up at the airport."

Through Kraig, I felt that we had lived a lifetime with Jacques. The mystical bond of brotherhood that united them demanded that he be present for the celebration of Kraig's life. We did not as yet understand what this bond meant for Jacques and his ministry. For the moment, silence surrounded us as the tiny grain that had fallen to the ground lay hidden in secret.

Chapter IX

A Time to Mourn (Eccles. 34)

Death can take away shiny, golden blond hair; it can take away the brightest, bluest eyes I have ever seen, and a smile that lights up the world; it can take away a pair of legs that used to run and jump and climb; it can even take away the spoken "I love yous" that melted my heart. But it can never take away love. Just as the love for your children grows with each passing day so, also, that love continues to increase through death into eternal life. I love Kraig more today than I did yesterday or the day before. With love, there is no beginning or end.

The evening following Kraig's death, Tony Fleo, head of Family Ministry at our parish, called and offered to help in any way possible. We met with Tony and Father Gray the following morning at the funeral home. With quiet compassion, Tony carefully guided us through the painful yet necessary process. There is so much involved in arranging for a funeral. Our whole family participated in the plans. I believe the time spent in these preparations provided an emotional outlet and helped to soften the harshness of reality, if only for a little while.

In the afternoon, Bridget Toro, our parish cantor, came to the house to go over the music. I had already contacted her to ask if she could sing at the vigil and funeral Mass. From the day Bridget approached me with prayers to Padre Pio, I knew she was united with me in unceasing prayer for a miracle. For Bridget, this alliance created a deep, emotional attachment to Kraig, so much so, I wondered if it might be too difficult for her to sing. When I told her of Kraig's death, she wept with me, but at the same time assured me that she would be available for whenever and whatever we needed.

In choosing the hymns, Mike and I both wanted Bridget to sing "Mother Beloved" at Kraig's Mass. Pop dearly loved this beautiful tribute to the Blessed Mother, and it had taken on a significant role in the important events of our family life. Mike and I chose it for our wedding Mass, and it was sung for the funeral Masses for both mom and pop. I wondered also if "The Wind Beneath My Wings," while not strictly within liturgical guidelines, would be suitable to sing at the vigil. Knowing how much it meant to me personally, Tony told Bridget it would be perfectly acceptable. I asked if she would mind singing it once again at the cemetery. Smiling tenderly, she nodded her head and readily agreed to my request.

Programs had to be put together for the vigil

and the Mass. We asked Tony if it was possible to include a picture of Kraig. Although this is now done regularly in our parish, Kraig's was the first funeral where a picture was incorporated into the programs. Tony contacted Valerie, the organist, who just happened to have software on her computer that could not only design text for each program but could crop and fit in Kraig's photograph.

For Mike and me, the most important consideration in all these preparations was to help our family and friends reflect on the joy of Kraig's entrance into heaven. We did not want people, especially children who would be present, to dwell on the tragic loss. It was to this end that Tony's help was invaluable. His experience enabled him to offer many wonderful suggestions. The theme we had selected came from the Gospel of Mark, chapter 10, verses 13-16: "Let the children come to me and do not hinder them. It is to just such as these that the kingdom of God belongs." We wanted those words printed beneath Kraig's picture, too.

Kraig's body would lie in repose in a small room off the atrium of the church. The casket would remain closed, with his second grade class picture resting on it. Tony would attend to all the details. Mike and I prepared an obituary. How could we capture the impact of Kraig's life on so many in so few words? It simply was not possible.

In the end, we merely tried to express what he meant to all of us:

Kraig James Frick entered everlasting life in heaven on September 17, 1996, at 3:00 PM., the Hour of Divine Mercy . . . Kraig is the dearly beloved son of Karyl and Mike Frick, and the treasured youngest brother of Luke, Bri, Ginger; Klaire, Karl and Dan Frick, and the brother-in-law of Regina Frick . . . He lived a short but joy-filled life to the fullest . . . All who have been touched by Kraig on this earth have been truly blessed.

The day before the vigil, our devoted friend Meg returned to Dallas with her family. Jacques arrived the following day. It turned out his plane landed about an hour before the vigil was scheduled to begin. When Mike left to pick him up at the airport, it suddenly dawned on him that we had only been in Jacques' company on two occasions. We had never heard him speak publicly, yet we had prevailed upon him to give a talk at the vigil and the homily at the Mass.

When Jacques arrived at the house with Mike, there was barely enough time to change and get ready. We wanted him to sleep in Kraig's room. While showing him where to put his belongings, I quickly said,

"Jacques, you know how busy I was in caring

for Kraig. I have had very little time to tell people in detail how we met. Will you be able to do that at the funeral Mass?"

With that all-engaging smile I remembered so well, he replied,

"Karyl, don't you worry. I'll take care of that."

When we arrived at All Saints Catholic Church, the atrium was bursting with floral arrangements. Tony had also set up a long table filled with family pictures and mementos of Kraig. There were ribbons and awards from all the sports Kraig had participated in, and even a soccer ball signed by all of his teammates. Kraig's moose, Biggie, was prominently positioned in the center of the table. It was perfect!

This was all Tony's idea, so that people who had not known Kraig would have a better understanding of who he was.

Mike held onto me tightly as we approached the room with Kraig's body. Meg and Jacques followed behind with our children. The casket was opened for our private viewing and we all knelt down together in prayer. It was so real and, at the same time, so unreal. We had placed one little moose and Kraig's rosary inside the casket. While standing next to me, Jacques turned and whispered,

"Karyl, would it be alright if I exchanged my crown for Kraig's rosary?"

The crown that Jacques referred to is that which is traditionally worn with the Franciscan habit: a seven-decade rosary with a large crucifix. Mike and I, so deeply touched by this heartfelt gesture, watched in awe as Jacques removed this beautiful rosary from the cincture of his habit and gently placed it into Kraig's hands in the coffin. Then he took the small rosary that Kraig had made in the second grade and slipped it into his pocket. Kraig's rosary was far from perfect, made of plastic beads and lots of string, but it was made with his own little hands.

Tony Fleo, who was standing in the back of the room, walked forward to close the casket before we processed into the church. Mike picked up Kraig's picture from atop the casket and handed it to me. I clutched it to my heart and together we walked down the center aisle of the church to an easel that had been set up on the side of the altar. Before placing it onto the easel, I lovingly kissed the picture while Mike stood with his arm around me. Then we turned and walked to our pew, genuflected and sat down. Tony later told us that such dignity, under the most difficult circumstance imaginable, set a beautiful example to everyone present.

Jacques stood up to speak.

"As I was preparing my talk for this evening, I had something that can only be described as a powerful, spiritual experience happen to me. It was not a vision; yet, I saw everything so clearly in my mind. Suddenly, I could see all these children running toward Jesus; not just a few ~ but many. In the middle of all these children, I saw a pair of moose antlers. I thought to myself: moose antlers? Just then, I could see Kraig carrying a moose, and the next thing I knew, he was sitting on the lap of Jesus, smiling and welcoming all the children."

For those who had no way of knowing, Jacques tried to explain briefly how attached Kraig was to his moose family. It was amusing and charming all at the same time. As his talk drew to a close, he ended with a surprising and touching plea.

"Kraig had a favorite prayer, one he had written as a school assignment before he became ill. It's a very simple prayer: *Lord, please help the people who need it most.* It would be a wonderful tribute to Kraig if perhaps we could establish a memorial fund in his name . . . "

Mike and I had it in the back of our minds that we would like to do something special in Kraig's name, but had not as yet formulated a concrete plan. Jacques' eloquence that night at the vigil gave birth to the Kraig Frick Memorial Fund, with Kraig's prayer as its official anthem. Shortly after the funeral, we began the fund with money Kraig had donated himself. During his illness, it was tough getting him to take his medicine so we made a game out of it. For every dose of medicine he took, he was awarded a small amount of money.

We told him he could use his "earnings" to buy baseball cards at the end of each week. Instead, he let his stash accumulate in a little jar and this became the starter seed for the fund. Since the day of his funeral, Kraig's prayer, written on lined paper, is kept on our kitchen table and we say it, along with grace, every day.

When the vigil ended, Mike and I stood in the back of the church thanking all who had taken the time to come. Jacques came out to the atrium and, like a magnet, began to attract a crowd. People continued to line up, hoping for a chance to speak to him personally. We marveled at the ease with which he greeted so many new faces and the gracious way he responded to questions. He stood for almost three hours without ever looking tired or anxious to get away.

Before going home, we took the family back to say our evening prayers with Kraig. When we were finished, one by one, the kids walked over to say goodnight to Kraig. As we turned to leave, we were surprised to see Tony Fleo in the room. He walked over to me and said:

"Karyl, I worked very hard to insure a beautiful liturgy for this evening, but just now, I have witnessed a personal liturgy that far surpasses anything I could have planned. Obviously, yours is a family accustomed to praying together, and I will never forget what I saw here tonight. I consider it a great grace to have served you."

We were deeply touched by his kind words and so grateful for all he had done behind the scenes. Without ever once being obtrusive, Tony managed to see to our every need. Nothing escaped his attention. When we were standing for so long in the reception line and I began to feel thirsty, suddenly he appeared with a glass of water! How could we ever thank him enough?

The morning of the funeral was bleak and dreary. The overcast sky matched the mood of all the mourners filing into All Saints Catholic Church. No matter what we might have been feeling over our loss, Mike and I wanted the overriding message of Kraig's funeral Mass to be faith, hope, and love. All the preparations and the music we had chosen were geared to that end.

In addition to our pastor and Father Gray, we had also invited the pastor of Mary Immaculate, and a priest who taught at both Jesuit Prep and Ursuline. We were delightfully surprised when the president, principal, and spiritual director of Jesuit Prep also joined in the procession. Altogether, there were seven priests plus Jacques on the altar, and the church was completely filled. Over and above family and close friends, the friends of every one of our children were there, plus many of Kraig's classmates.

Bridget Toro had never been in better voice. Our eyes met when she stood up to lead the responsorial psalm, "The Lord is my light and my salvation . . ." As her magnificent voice filled the church, I repeated the words in my heart in silent prayer.

I gazed up at Jacques on the altar, the lone Franciscan, and still a seminarian. Soon, he would have to step forward in front of all these long-time Jesuit priests and give the homily. Mike and I both knew he would be wonderful. We were right. In a matter of minutes, everyone in the church, including the Jesuits, were hanging on his every word. After introducing himself, Jacques shared the story of how we met.

"I was in Colorado on retreat," he began. "We Franciscans are such a tight-knit group, I did not pay much attention when this woman, who I thought was just another tourist, walked into the chapel that day. St. Malo's is such a distinctively beautiful church, and visitors from all over the world come by daily. We had just finished praying for my father, who was dying from an inoperable brain tumor, before she entered the chapel. Later, during Mass, Karyl stood up and requested prayers for her son, who was also suffering with an inoperable brain tumor. Being in such a vulnerable state myself, I thought, How can this be? Who is this woman? What I didn't realize at the time was that God was preparing a series of remarkable coincidences, so that when Karyl and I met, we would form an immediate bond. She took me home that day to meet her family, but especially Kraig.

Of Moose and Miracles

"I can say in all honesty that Kraig was a child I loved from the first minute I met him. Many of you may know of Kraig's love of moose. Let me tell you, if you ever have the chance to go to the Frick cabin in Colorado, you will soon discover that everything from doorposts to dishes is in the moose mode. Part of the moose mementos in the cabin include an empty Moosehead Beer carton perched on the mantle. Moose were very much a part of my own background and childhood in Canada. Moosehead Beer just happens to be brewed in New Brunswick, the province where I was raised. I never cease to marvel at God's wonderful sense of humor. It was the beer carton that completely convinced me that my meeting the Frick family was part of some greater plan. And I was right!

"Mike and Karyl are so deeply embedded in my heart, it's as if I've always known them. Karyl's faith was the catalyst that inspired me to pray in earnest for a miracle for my father and for Kraig. Together, we formed a prayer partnership that eventually spread around the globe. Just weeks ago, my father was instantaneously healed!"

The congregation let out a collective sigh. Jacques paused dramatically for a moment, and then continued.

"Both Karyl and Mike want you to know that it is Kraig who received the greater miracle. He has been perfected in heaven where the celebration of life is eternal . . ."

Jacques' homily was exactly the kind of positive message that Mike and I wanted for everyone attending Kraig's resurrection liturgy. He realized our deepest wishes.

After the Mass, our children served as the pall bearers. They would not think of allowing anyone else to perform this final task for their little brother. As we walked out of church, Father Phil Postell, the president of Jesuit, approached us and said,

"When I die, I only hope that I have as loving pall bearers as Kraig has today."

Mike and I were escorted to a waiting limousine, while a long procession of cars lined up for the ride to the cemetery. We had police escorts to keep the traffic flowing. Along the route, there was a lot of construction taking place. All the construction workers, who had no idea who Kraig was, turned to face the procession of cars and, with hard hats in hand, bowed their heads in quiet reverence. I had never seen anything like it.

Once inside the cemetery, the kids lined up on either side of the hearse. The minute the door was opened, the sun burst out and illuminated Kraig's little casket. It nearly took my breath away. The sun remained in place during the entire prayer service.

A tent had been set up at the gravesite, and folding chairs were arranged in rows for the family. A great number of people came to the cemetery;

they stood in solemn silence around the grave. The priests were positioned in the front of the casket and, once again, repeated the prayers for the repose of Kraig's soul. Our pastor then sprinkled the casket with holy water and imparted a final blessing. The crowd remained standing in hushed silence. With the angelic strains of the harp in the background, Bridget Toro stood up and sang *our* song, Kraig's and mine. The harp was such a lovely surprise, another wonderful touch arranged for by Tony Fleo. With my eyes closed, I silently mouthed the words, *'Did you ever know that you're my hero?'* along with Bridget. I thought about all the people present and realized that Kraig was not only my hero. The indomitable courage he showed throughout his illness made him a hero to everyone who knew him.

After the final blessing, throngs of people, many of whom were children, quietly came over to pay their final respects to our family. Martin, our neighbor and Kraig's dear little friend, was sobbing as he walked toward us. We reached out to embrace him and tried to assure him that Kraig was happier now than he had ever been.

Our beloved son Kraig lived for only nine years. Naturally, we would have liked to see him grow up, graduate from school, perhaps marry, or become a priest, or follow whatever his dream might have been. Instead, we witnessed all of Kraig's life ~ and what a remarkable life it was! He was born on his father's birthday. He made his First Communion on the Feast of Divine Mercy. He died on the Feast of St. Francis's stigmata, at exactly 3:00 P.M., the Hour of Divine Mercy ~ and the day of his burial just happened to be the Feast of Padre Pio's stigmata.

Shortly after the funeral, I was going through Kraig's things when I came across one of his school papers. It was an assignment for his religion class, one in which he had had to write down the date of his baptism and the names of his godparents. I looked down at the date in utter amazement. Kraig was baptized on October 4, the feast day of St. Francis of Assisi!

From the day Jacques had entered our lives, it was as if we were meeting St. Francis at every turn. It happened again at Kraig's vigil. Amid all the gorgeous bouquets that came, one in particular stood out. I have attended many funerals in the past where statues of the Blessed Mother were included with flowers, but this arrangement caught my attention because St. Francis was standing in the center of it. Naturally, we assumed Jacques had sent it, but it actually came from one of our old friends who had no notion of the St. Francis connection.

Once again, I was seized with an incredible awe before the design of heaven, and our connection with Jacques grew less mysterious as it grew more wonderful.

Chapter X

A Time to Be Silent (Eccles. 3:7)

Good friends are a blessing in times of sorrow; but their comforting presence must eventually make way for the gradual healing one has to face alone. Meg and I shared a tearful goodbye; then it was time for Jacques to leave. His participation in all the funeral services had been such a comfort to the whole family, it was difficult to let him go, but he had to get back to Maryland to complete the final portion of his studies. I told him to be sure to give our love and best wishes to his mother and father and to stay in touch with us.

Getting back to the business of everyday living was something we each had to do in our own way, but all of us were united in our love and support for each other. Without Kraig, our lives would never be the same, but in his memory, we would continue to celebrate life. We were grateful that we now had our own little saint in heaven to help us over the rough spots.

As for me, I had good days; I had bad days. There were moments of such torment that I feared whether or not I would make it. I recall one especially difficult day. I was sitting alone on Kraig's bed, feeling empty. I picked up Moosie and held him close to my heart. All I could think of was the joy on Kraig's face that Christmas when he spotted this gift that I had bought purely on impulse. I broke into uncontrollable sobs and, as I lay there with my eyes closed, I could see Kraig's face, all aglow and laughing, just like he used to be when we played our silly game, "Kraig, you make me . . ." In anguish, I buried my face in his pillow and cried out,

"You know, Kraig, you're going to have to figure out a way to make me happy. . . Again."

My plea was answered when Luke and Regina presented us with our first grandchild. Names had long ago been selected, but Luke and Regina surprised us when they announced that our grandson would be named Garrett Kraig Frick. He was born on November 1, the Feast of All Saints, and I could not help but wonder if our little saint in heaven had anything to do with that!

The first holidays following the death of a loved one are tough, but we all made the effort to focus on the joy of the season. On Christmas morning, as I sat watching the kids enthusiastically opening their presents, Mike placed a small, beautifully wrapped package into my lap. After Kraig died, I had wanted a piece of jewelry bearing his picture to wear all the time. I remembered that when Luke and Bri were born, the hospital gave us small plastic charms with their pictures encased inside. My mother had taken them to a jeweler and had each of the pictures embossed onto a gold disc for her charm bracelet. I decided to take a picture of Kraig to a jeweler, along with Mom's bracelet, and ask if a similar charm could be made for me. He said it could be done, but it would have to be sent out. A week later, the jeweler called Mike saying he had already ordered the charm, but found another company who, for just a few dollars more, could make one that could also be engraved ~ were we interested? Mike said yes, but still wanted the first charm to present to me on Christmas day. I fought back the tears as I lifted the charm from the box and looked over at Mike to thank him.

"Don't thank me," he whispered. "Thank Kraig. This is from him."

We had always taken the children to Florida right after Christmas and this year would be no different. We left the very next day with plans to return to Dallas the first week in January. The kids had a wonderful time, and the change of scenery was good for all of us. On the day of our departure, as we stood at the gate, an announcement came over the loud speaker:

"Ladies and Gentlemen, we regret to inform you that we have overbooked this flight. We will be happy to offer a free round trip ticket to anywhere in the United States to anyone who is willing to give up their seat in exchange for a later flight."

Mike and I looked at each other and smiled. With no compelling reason to get home immediately, why not set ourselves up with some free tickets for the future? We signaled to the kids who got into the excitement with us. It was like celebrating Christmas all over again.

The second charm took quite a while to complete, but it was worth the wait. The jeweler did an incredible job. Kraig's picture was set on the face of a large, round 14K gold disc trimmed in gold filigree. On the backside, Kraig's signature was reproduced from a school paper he had signed when he was learning to write in cursive. The day I went in to pick up the charm, the jeweler said,

"By the way, Mrs. Frick, I have one other charm with your son's picture. Would you like to have it?"

Would I like to have it? With Kraig's picture on it, of course, I would. However, I was a bit puzzled. How did there happen to be two charms? The jeweler explained that the place that had designed the first charm had mistakenly made two. He placed it into my hand and told me it was mine to keep. Two for the price of one! The idea occurred to me that perhaps, at a later date, I could have something made for Mike with that charm.

I wear the gold medallion bearing Kraig's picture and signature on a chain around my neck every day. It is a constant reminder that he is still with me. It also keeps Kraig alive for others. Many times, perfect strangers have approached me, asking if the boy on the charm is my son. When I answer yes, they usually say something like, "He must be a very special boy." My response is always, "Yes, he is indeed!" Most people let it go at that, but there have been a few who have delved more deeply. I certainly do nothing to encourage questions, but if someone asks about Kraig, I tell them what happened. To my surprise, there have even been times when the charm made it possible for me to comfort others. In those instances, the people who had asked about Kraig turned out to be suffering heartaches of their own, usually involving a child. With the help of God's grace, not to mention Kraig's intercession, I have been able to offer a soothing word.

By the end of January, I began to experience great difficulty with my left side. It became so bothersome that I had to return to the hospital to have the pins removed. This procedure brought some relief, but could not stop the continuing deterioration of the hip and the consequent need for more surgery. Needless to say, I was feeling pretty low about this. To my surprise, a little "touch of Jacques" lightened my load. The day I returned home from the hospital, a package arrived from him. It was a beautiful Lennox statue of Jesus holding a little boy in his lap, with another child at his side. The note inside said,

Dear Karyl,

This statue reminded me of Kraig. When I saw it on a friar's desk in my community, I told him about Kraig and how we had met. After I was finished, Father Gene took it and gave it to me and said: This belongs to the Frick family. So here it is. When you look at this, think of the Gospel reading at Kraig's resurrection liturgy. I love you very much.

Your brother in Christ and in St. Kraig,
Jacques, OFM

The statue could not have come at a better time. That evening, Mike and I called Jacques to thank him personally, and also to get the full name of the priest who gave it to him so we could acknowledge his thoughtfulness. We talked about many things, mostly about the upcoming ordination. Jacques was counting the days. He said he hoped so much that we would be able to share this glorious day with him, and he could not wait for us to meet his father. As a further enticement, he hastened to add,

"Karyl, you have to come. Kraig is going to be with me. I just know it!"

"Well, we already have travel vouchers for five roundtrip tickets," I said jokingly, explaining what had happened in Florida. Jacques immediately responded with,

"Kraig arranged that purposely because he

wants the whole family to come."

We broke into gales of laughter, but deep down, each of us pondered the possibility that Kraig might have actually intervened. I tried to convey to Jacques how grateful I was that he was allowing Kraig to play a part in his ministry, and with characteristic humility, he insisted that the blessing was his.

There was another matter I wanted to talk about, and now seemed to be the right moment. Mike and I wanted to give Jacques something very special for his ordination. It was a delicate matter because we certainly did not want to intrude in any way with plans his family might already have, but the two of us had discussed the possibility of giving Jacques his chalice. When we mentioned this, Jacques was astounded.

"This is Divine Providence at work again!" he sighed. "My family has decided to give me the ciborium. I wondered about a chalice, but then I realized that God would take care of it. And, now, the two of you are asking me if it's all right? It's more than all right ~ it's perfect! My only stipulation is that you pick out a chalice you think Kraig would choose if he were here. Please do not buy an expensive one . . . and there's one more thing: I want Kraig's name, the date he was born, and the date he went to heaven engraved on it."

We made no attempt to conceal our excitement and told Jacques we would take care of it as soon as possible.

To provide a newly ordained priest with the vessel that would contain the precious blood of Jesus was such an honor for us, it defied description. We chose a simple gold chalice with a matching paten and carefully printed out on paper the inscriptions we wanted to be engraved on each piece. In the center of the paten, a small gold plate, we wanted the words "In Union with the Faith, Hope and Love of the Body of Christ." On the bottom of the chalice, we wanted "Jacques LaPointe, OFM, May 17, 1997" to appear above the words "In Union with the Faith, Hope and Love of the Blood of Christ," and underneath that we wanted "Kraig James Frick, September 9,1987-September 17,1996."

We had to wait a couple of weeks before both pieces would be ready. I could hardly contain myself until the day arrived. The chalice was beautiful, but when I turned it upside down to view the engraving, I was a bit dismayed. It looked very good, but I had just assumed that the inscription would be placed in a semi-circular fashion with words on the top and bottom of the stem. Instead, all the engraving was placed on the topside. Even though this bothered me somewhat, I made a conscious decision not to allow anything to spoil my happiness and accepted both chalice and paten with words of praise and gratitude for a job well done. Little did I realize at the time that God has a marvelous way of transforming a minor mistake into a major masterpiece.

A few weeks passed. Then, one day, I was inspired with an idea that hit me like a thunderbolt. I ran back to my room and grabbed that "extra" charm with Kraig's picture and placed it on the empty space at the bottom of the chalice. It looked like it had been made for the chalice! Mike could not believe it when I showed him. We took it back to a jeweler to have the charm bonded on and when it was finished, the chalice was exquisite.

It would be another six weeks before the ordination, and I wanted to hold onto the chalice for a while before sending it to Jacques. In the meantime, Kraig's teacher had asked me to come and speak to one of the third grade classes. I thought showing them the chalice would be an excellent opportunity for me to explain that Kraig, though physically gone, would always be united with them in prayer. Children are so wonderful, so innocent and unafraid to share their thoughts. As soon as I arrived, they eagerly showed me how they had kept Kraig's desk and locker intact. They also wanted me to be sure to know that Kraig was included in everything they did in class. I was overwhelmed with affection for each and every one of them. After a brief talk, I passed the chalice to each child so they could actually see Kraig's name appearing below Jacques'. Some of them wanted to hold it; others just wanted to touch it. The teacher then proposed a class activity by asking all the children to make a card for Jacques' ordination. I told them how happy it would make Jacques and that I would personally deliver their good wishes. The children's cards were priceless. One child wrote, "Gee, I hope the fingerprints come off the chalice." I could already hear Jacques' laughter.

Chapter XI

A Time to Love (Eccles. 3:6)

There are certain incomparable milestones in each person's life and being part of Jacques' ordination definitely marked an experience that Mike and I will never forget. We were already excited at the prospect of attending our first ordination; we were overjoyed when Jacques asked us to participate in the ceremony by joining his parents in presenting the Offertory gifts during the Mass.

With Bri living so close to Hartford, I wanted to leave Texas a few days before the ordination in order to spend some time with him. Klaire was able to go on ahead with me. The day after our arrival just happened to be my birthday, so Bri took us to Martha's Vineyard to celebrate. Mike and the rest of the family, including our newest member, Garrett Kraig, flew into Boston on May 16, and early the next morning, we all set out by car for Connecticut.

The weather was gorgeous with blue skies, white puffy clouds and bright sunshine. As we drove through Hartford, I admired the colorful azaleas embellishing many of the homes along the route to St. Patrick-St. Anthony Church where Jacques was to be ordained. (That was another first ~ a church with two names!) Delicate spring blossoms abounded everywhere, filling the air with their sweet perfume. I thought how fitting it was for Jacques to begin his new life on such a day as this.

We arrived at the church well in advance of the ceremony, but many of the seats were already filled. We quickly filed into a pew. I opened the program and gently poked Mike, pointing to our names which appeared under "Gift Bearers." We also noted a special message that read, "As we celebrate this Eucharist, Jacques asks that you remember the intentions of Ricky LaPointe, Francine Lecierc and Kraig Frick." Ricky LaPointe was Jacques' nephew who had died in a tragic accident in December. Francine Lecierc was Jacques' thirty year old cousin who had recently died of cancer.

Sacred music suddenly resounded throughout the church and the congregation stood to join with the choir in the processional hymn, "We Rely On The Power Of God." Everyone turned to face the center aisle as a long line of Franciscans led the ceremonial procession, followed by the bishop, two Franciscan priests who would concelebrate the Mass, a deacon and, finally, Jacques. He was radiant, with a joy beyond words on his face and in his eyes. As he walked slowly past our pew, he caught sight of us. Our eyes locked immediately and even if I had wanted to, I could never have concealed my excitement. The purpose for which he was born was about to be fulfilled, and in God's mysterious plan, we were there to share in its blessings.

As the procession reached the altar and each man took his place, I looked at Jacques standing there and wondered what was going through his mind. The bishop greeted everyone warmly and asked that we join our prayers with his for Jacques, not just for this joyous day of ordination, but for every day of his life in the priesthood.

Of course, having been raised a Catholic, I knew a little something about the sacrament of Holy Orders. I understood that a bishop, as part of the apostolic line, hands on to the candidate the "gift of the Holy Spirit," commissioning him to go forth to proclaim the Gospel of Jesus Christ and administer the life-giving sacraments of the Church. Nonetheless, attending my first ordination was a greater catechism than anything I had received in the past. The majestic nature of this ceremony, rich with symbolism and tradition, moved me beyond words. The splendor of the Mass has always impressed me, but this particular celebration transcended any I had ever seen. I felt as if I had been transported to heaven and stood rejoicing with all the saints, especially our own little saint, Kraig.

After the bishop's greeting, there followed a ritual of election and examination of the candidate. Jacques was presented to the people, and his readiness for ordination was declared. On receiving this confirmation, the bishop officially accepted him. By this beautiful action, the priesthood is seen as both personal and communal, a gift to the man and to the Church.

The rite of ordination took place after the homily. Having made a promise of obedience to the bishop, Jacques lay fully prostrate on the floor before the altar while the congregation and choir sang the Litany of the Saints. The history of our faith, into which each of us has been inscribed by baptism, unfolded itself through the names of holy men and women who gave witness as bishops and doctors, virgins and martyrs, spouses and religious. I recognized some of these names as my spiritual friends to whom I had turned in the past year for light and consolation. I realized how great, how wide, is our family of faith. Whether in heaven above or earth below, we are one family.

After the litany, Jacques approached the bishop and, kneeling before him, received ordination. The bishop laid his hands on Jacques' head and prayed quietly. Such a simple gesture, with such enormous meaning. Then, the new priest was clothed with the chasuble and stole ~ gifts from his parents. Finally, the bishop anointed Jacques' hands with oil as a sign of the sacred power he now possessed to consecrate bread and wine into the Body and Blood of the Lord.

As the time for the Offertory drew near, a Franciscan walked up to Jacques' parents to escort them to the back of the church. Mike and I followed to a table that had been set up for the gifts. We stood in silence as the Franciscan placed in our hands the different items to be presented. I was the last one in line. He handed me the chalice and paten! As we proceeded to the altar, the bishop, along with another priest and Jacques, now *Father* Jacques, came forward to greet us and receive the gifts. My eyes met Jacques' and, for that fleeting moment, it was as if we could see into each other's soul. I carefully placed the chalice and paten into the hands of the bishop. Every time Jacques, as a priest, elevated that chalice after the words of consecration, with the precious blood of God's only begotten Son within it, he would also be lifting the image of our beloved son. This realization hit me with such force that I could barely breathe. As we turned to depart, I felt like I was floating on air and wondered if I would be able to walk back to my seat. Fortunately, Mike was there to hold my hand. The bishop blessed the paten and the chalice, reciting aloud the ritual prayers prescribed by the Church, and then formally presented them to Jacques as an offering of the holy people of God.

Mass concluded with a solemn blessing by the

bishop. Then everyone broke into a rousing recessional hymn as the Franciscans lined up to lead the procession out of the church. Father Jacques LaPointe came behind his brothers, beaming jubilantly as he acknowledged friends and relatives on both sides of the aisle. The minute we emerged from the church, he ran up to us extending his arms. For a moment we enjoyed a "hug fest." Then, like a child who cannot wait to reveal a secret, Jacques said breathlessly,

"I have something I want to show you."

I watched as he dug through the beautiful white robes adorning his brown habit until he found the right pocket. He clasped the object he was searching for and, with a clenched fist, he stretched forth his hand. I could not imagine what he was holding. Slowly, he turned his hand over and opened his fingers to reveal Kraig's little homemade rosary. Tears began to well up in my eyes as I pulled Mike over to see.

"I want you both to know that this rosary was next to my heart all during the ceremony. There is much more I have to say, but I'll save it for later when we can talk alone."

The Franciscans had invited everyone who attended the ordination to a large reception area in the friary that was located next to the church. Jacques' parents and some of his close relatives had already gathered together in a private room. The people outside kept coming up to congratulate

Jacques. Mike and I decided to head over to the reception area to find a table where we could all sit together. A while later, Jacques came in looking for us. Garrett Kraig had fallen asleep in Regina's arms and the first thing Jacques did was to walk over and place his newly ordained hands on the baby's head. He prayed in silence for several minutes, then turned to me and whispered,

"That was a very special blessing I just imparted ~ it came from Kraig."

What a precious gift this was to all of us. I seized the opportunity to try to express what it was like for me to be the one who presented the chalice and paten to the bishop. Mike spoke up saying, "I'll bet you arranged for that, didn't you, Jacques?"

Shaking his head and looking right at me, he said,

"I had absolutely nothing to do with it. I guess that makes it even better, doesn't it?"

"Oh, yes!" I exclaimed.

Without further ado, he grabbed both of us and announced,

"Come, you must meet my parents!"

We were weaving in and out of circles of people while Jacques, still holding onto me, stopped all along the route to engage in a few words of conversation. When we finally made our way out of the room, he squeezed my hand, I motioned to Mike, and the three of us practically ran down the stairs of the friary. His parents were standing together in a room downstairs. Jacques called to them, and as they turned to face us, I was struck once again by the observation I had made in church ~ Jacques was the image of his father!

I already had so much affection for these people whom I had never met. At last, I would have the opportunity to express my feelings. But Fernand was one step ahead of me. He walked right up to me and took my hands in his. His eyes were moist with tears as he said,

"I would not be here if it were not for you!"

We embraced and then he turned to introduce me to his wife Theresa, a small, soft-spoken woman. Having been united together for so long in prayer, it was more like a reunion than a first meeting. We talked a lot about Kraig, and I told them how Jacques had won him over instantly. Knowing their son, they laughed heartily when I described the antics he went through just to impress Kraig.

The evening reception was really something special, with guests present from all over the world. Tables set for a formal dinner filled the large room. Jacques started the festivities by asking a representative from each table to stand up, give their name, tell where they were from and, perhaps, share a few sentiments. He hastened to add, "No personal stuff ~ I don't want anyone to embarrass me!" One by one, all around the room, people introduced themselves, their spouses and children, and then proceeded to relate a poignant, oftentimes hilarious, story involving Jacques. It was great fun, and Jacques made no attempt to conceal his delight at some of the clever banter being shared at his expense. In fact, his laughter could be heard above everyone else's. Ours was the last table. I had no sooner stood up to make the introductions than Jacques jumped up out of his seat and gently interrupted.

"I want each of you here to know that one of the reasons this day has been so perfect for me is because this is the day Karyl and Mike have been united physically with my parents and all of our family. For many months, we have been united in prayer and now we are finally together."

The room broke into applause. Most of the people there knew about Fernand's miracle and the connection with Kraig. Then, Jacques proceeded to share a few personal details about our first meeting in Colorado and all that had happened since. I have never known anybody with a gift for describing things as eloquently as Jacques does. Everyone in the room was spellbound. When he finished, he headed for our table with his arms spread open, and I ran right to him and said,

"You just keep doing this!"

Applause broke out again as Jacques escorted

me back to my seat.

I didn't think it was possible for anything to top this incredible evening, but I was wrong. When the dinner was over and people were beginning to depart, Jacques asked to speak to me privately. We found an empty table over in the corner, and when we sat down, I noticed Jacques was holding onto Kraig's rosary. Fingering the beads, he began,

"Karyl, when I entered the seminary, we were a class of eleven men, but as time went on, all of them left except me. I prayed harder than I ever have, asking God: Why am I the only one? I was lonely and wanted so much to have at least one other seminarian with whom I could share my priesthood. This morning, during the Litany of the Saints, while I was lying prostrate on the altar, Kraig was beside me. Oh yes, I know what you're thinking ~ his rosary was pressed against my heart, but I am talking about the presence of Kraig himself. He was there! In fact, I was so certain, I literally inched my way over to allow a space for him next to me."

I could not respond. It was impossible for me to even speak. Jacques continued to explain.

"It was more than not being alone on that altar. Remember the day of my solemn vows when Kraig was so sick and called out my name at precisely the same time I saw his image in the host? At the time, I thought God was revealing to me that Kraig was somehow mysteriously linked to my vocation.

Now, I am convinced that God was laying the groundwork that day for a ministry that would far exceed anything I could have imagined. It came to me when I was face down on the altar that Kraig was not only present but, in answer to my prayer, God had sent me a brother priest. Karyl, there is no doubt in my mind that Kraig was ordained with me."

"Jacques, I don't even know what to say!"

"That day of my solemn vows, I also pondered on the fact that while my father had no trace of cancer and was recovering from a heart attack and stroke, Kraig was getting much worse. At the time, I had such a strong sense that somehow these circumstances were interrelated, and now I am convinced that Kraig was taking my father's cancer with him. Kraig was a victim soul, and I believe that God will use him more powerfully now than would have been possible had he remained on earth. Do you remember telling me that you had hoped that maybe one day Kraig would become a priest? Looking back now, I believe it was already settled. God had chosen the companion I prayed for, one who in time and eternity would be ordained with me and share in my priesthood. There were other signs, too, signs that pointed to the conclusion I was already reaching. I thought about how it came to pass that you and Mike ended up presenting me with a chalice, how the jeweler had mistakenly made two charms of Kraig, and then, how the engraver had arranged the inscriptions allowing a blank space that was custom-made for that charm . . . I could go on and on, but you get the point. Karyl, believe me, Kraig's ordination is as real to me as the sound of your voice is right now, but it takes faith to believe in such a gift. We must continue to believe that God will reveal His power to us by allowing Kraig not merely to be a part of, but to actively participate in whatever direction my priesthood takes me."

As I listened to Jacques, the pieces of the puzzle seemed to fall into place at last. I drew a deep breath as months of anguished questioning dissolved into peace.

"Oh, Jacques, I cannot even begin to describe how I feel . . . This has been one of the happiest days of my life, and you have just given me the most glorious gift I can think of this side of heaven. How can I ever thank you? How can I ever thank God?"

Chapter XII

A Time to Build (Eccles. 3:3)

Mike and I returned to Dallas on an incredible high. We could not stop talking about Kraig's mystical ordination. We were trying to understand just what it would mean and how it would play out. As thrilling as it was, it was also extremely humbling. For God to bring such joy out of unbearable pain was for us proof positive of His infinite goodness.

Scripture says, "The favors of the Lord are not exhausted . . . They are renewed each morning . . ." The greatest manifestation of this scriptural promise exists in the Holy Sacrifice of the Mass. I make an effort to attend daily Mass, and since Jacques' ordination, every time the priest elevates the chalice, I place myself in union with Jacques and Kraig in thanksgiving to God for all of His blessings. Scripture also says, "At nightfall weeping enters in, but with the dawn rejoicing." We had passed through the night; now, realizing all that God was accomplishing in and through us, our hearts rejoiced.

Jacques left Hartford and returned briefly to his home parish in Canada to celebrate his first Mass. The pastor, along with a parish committee, put a beautiful liturgy together in his honor, but the thing that delighted Jacques the most was the participation of so many children. He wrote to tell us that he was convinced Kraig must have had a hand in that. All of Jacques' letters touch us with the beautiful simplicity of his words and the intimate manner in which he confides his heart to us. This letter was no exception. He closed by saying that in expressing his love for Mike and me, he was also assuring us of Kraig's continued and everlasting love for us and for our entire family.

We selfishly would have loved to keep Jacques close enough where we could visit him occasionally, but we had to accept the fact that God had other plans. Considering Jacques' skills and talent, it came as no surprise when he announced that he would be involved in missionary work in Japan. Referring to himself and Kraig as the "Moose Team," he promised to always keep us abreast of all the special graces he anticipated would come through their priestly partnership.

Jacques arrived in Tokyo on October 3, just in time to celebrate the feast of St. Francis of Assisi and also the thirtieth anniversary of the Franciscan chapel there. He told me that before reaching Japan, he and Kraig had celebrated Mass in New York, Rome and Assisi. In fact, Jacques was the last priest to celebrate Mass in the Basilica of Assisi before a major earthquake struck the area. When it happened, he was already on a bus heading for Milan to board the plane that would take him to Japan.

Our life in Dallas has entered a new phase. It's not just the loss of Kraig that makes everything different. Family life does not stand still. Luke and Regina are busy with a home and family of their own. Ginger lives and works in Ft. Worth, while Bri is back in Boston. Our daughter Klaire is getting ready to go away to college. Mike and I still have Karl and Dan at home, and we are still involved in the usual round of activities that goes along with raising a family. Sometimes, though, the house seems very quiet.

The Kraig Frick Memorial Fund, which began with a jar of Kraig's coins, has now reached universal proportions thanks to Jacques' expertise in fund raising. On a local level, generous contributions continue to pour in regularly. Kraig's prayer, "Lord, please help the people who need it most," has been adopted by his classmates as part of their morning devotions.

In addition to their personal contributions, Kraig's class also sponsored a Lenten project to collect money for the Franciscan mission in Pestel, Haiti. A friend of mine designed a flyer for the campaign with Kraig's picture and prayer in the upper left-hand corner. It also included photographs of the mission church and school, a snapshot of a Haitian child, and a group picture of the Franciscan community stationed there. In the middle of the flyer appeared the words "Please . . .help Kraig help the children of Haiti." Every student at Mary Immaculate School received a copy of the flier, and a large poster was made for display in the entrance hall of the school. Mike and I were overwhelmed by the enthusiasm these kids put into this project. Their efforts paid off handsomely. In recognition of the donations received, the Franciscans in Pestel have inscribed Kraig's name, along with that of Jacques' nephew, Ricky, on the baptismal font in their newly built church. In Dallas, a scholarship fund has been established in Kraig's name at All Saints Catholic School. I cannot help but marvel once again at how Divine Providence has revealed itself ~ Jacques received the grace to give his life to others while working with the poor in Haiti. Many years later, Haiti would be the site of Kraig Frick's first apostolic effort.

I will be forever grateful for the impact Kraig made on the lives of all of us in the family, but I simply was not prepared for the effect he has had and continues to have on others.

Bridget Toro experienced Kraig's help in a dramatic way the very day of his funeral. Bridget works as a speech therapist. Immediately after singing at the cemetery, she had to leave for work.

That evening, while driving home, she was reflecting on the events of the past few days ~ all so fresh in her mind. She was grateful to the Holy Spirit for carrying her through the vigil, the Mass and the burial. She pulled out a rosary from her purse to turn these thoughts into prayer. No sooner had she begun to pray, however, than she saw an out-of-control van in the oncoming lane. Bridget knew that the van, now airborne, was going to hit her. The thought flashed through her mind: I am going to die the day we buried Kraig! She closed her eyes and cried out in prayer for help. The van slammed into a light pole before hitting Bridget's van. Her vehicle spun around through three lanes of traffic finally stopping on the curb in the right lane, heading east, 180 degrees turned from the direction in which she had been going. The boy who hit her ended up, similarly, in the right lane heading west. They had totally reversed positions! Bridget had not hit the brakes ~ a moment of restraint which probably saved her life. Had she slowed down, the boy would have crashed right into her windshield. There were two other cars involved in the accident, both of which smashed into Bridget's van. She was struck with such force that the rear axle was ripped from her van; yet Bridget escaped with one broken rib and bruised knees. She firmly believes that God's angels and little Kraig Frick were by her side working a miracle for her and the other drivers. This was confirmed for her by people who were on the scene and shook their heads in disbelief when she got out of the van. Six people were involved in the three-car pile-up; miraculously, everyone walked away.

Other stories of Kraig's intercession, somewhat less dramatic, have also come to me. A woman, who had been deeply troubled with personal problems concerning her child turned to Kraig in prayer asking him to intercede on her son's behalf. The answer came with such remarkable speed, she felt compelled to share it with me. When such incidents come to my attention, they reinforce my faith in Kraig's mystical ordination. Our little saint, our priest, continues to reveal God's omnipotent love through other people.

Mike and I have had our own special experiences with Kraig. I sincerely believe that God speaks to people in a way they will understand. We have always been outdoor types, and we have tried to give all of our children a sense of appreciation for God's creative beauty in nature. Mike and I both believe that God has used our affinity with nature to reveal Kraig's presence to us. I am not certain when these experiences began, but Kraig's spirit has been made known to us at different times in the sudden appearances of either butterflies or cardinals. I wondered why butterflies were the means of communication until Jacques told me that the butterfly is a symbol of eternal life.

One day, shortly after leaving Mary Immaculate School, I was at an intersection waiting for the light to turn. I was talking to Mike on the car phone when, suddenly, a Monarch butterfly crossed right in front of my windshield. Another time, in Colorado, while Mike and I were visiting friends, we decided to take the children to a go-cart place. We had no sooner arrived, than a butterfly swooped down close to us. I reached out, and the butterfly softly landed on my hand and remained there until we got ready to leave. Only then did it fly away. Intuitively, I grasped that the butterfly had come as a message from Kraig, to let me know he was with us and enjoying the fun the boys were having on the go-carts.

The cemetery where Kraig is buried is within walking distance of our home. For a headstone, we chose a white marble cross and had it designed with an oval enclosure right in the center, large enough for a picture of Kraig. We placed a bench in front of his grave, and some neighbors brought over a bird feeder that hangs from a nearby tree. On bright days, in the late afternoon, the sun's rays shine down upon the headstone, and the cross glistens with the sparkling brilliance of diamonds. The setting is so peaceful that Mike and I like to go there sometimes to be quiet together and pray.

The first time I remember linking a cardinal with Kraig was at the cemetery. Ish, the little goldfish that had survived the aquarium disaster, finally died. We have lost many goldfish over the years, but the memory of what Ish symbolized for me during Kraig's illness made parting with it especially difficult. Mike and I decided to take the little goldfish over to the cemetery to bury it beside Kraig. While we were there, a cardinal came and hovered over us. It was not more than a few weeks later when Kraig's lizard, the one Meg had given to him on his last birthday, also died. Like Ish, we wanted to bury the lizard beside Kraig. As we worked to loosen the soil at the grave, once again, a cardinal appeared. Both thinking the same thing, we came to the conclusion that this was not mere happenstance. Thus it was that "Kardinal Kraig" entered our lives. Little did we know that this rendezvous with a cardinal was just the beginning.

One morning, we took the kids out to breakfast and afterwards drove over to the cemetery. We had no sooner arrived than I shouted,

"Look kids, there's Kardinal Kraig!"

The cardinal flew right to where we were standing and perched on the bird feeder. Karl walked over with his hand outstretched to where he could touch the feeder. The bird never flinched.

On the Memorial Day following Kraig's death, I was having a very tough time. It was one of those weepy days where no matter what direction I tried to focus my thoughts, I could not stop crying. I was sitting alone in the living room staring out at the patio when Kardinal Kraig flew down and landed on the back of a chair in full view. With tears still trickling down my cheeks, a memory of something

Kraig used to say popped into my mind.

"Mom, you're such a cry baby ~ you cry when you're sad and you cry when you're happy!"

Wiping away the tears, I cast my eyes upon the bird, still facing me as if waiting for some sort of acknowledgment. I broke into a great big smile and found myself saying,

"Kraig, you *do* make me . . .happy!"

Signs like these are not just willy-nilly. They seem to appear when we most need them, and not only that, they come in a way adapted to our individual needs and personalities. Take, for instance, the morning Mike got up and was rushing around to get ready for work. There were a lot of things going on at the office that day, and everything that could go wrong did. To top it off, he could not find his car keys. Exasperated, Mike kept retracing his steps, checking closets, drawers, anywhere and everywhere he thought he might have left them. He was standing in the kitchen gazing out the window and taking a mental inventory of his possessions when, out of nowhere, two cardinals appeared before his eyes. For Mike, the message was loud and clear ~ the pair of cardinals had to be a nudge from Kraig for the "September the 9th guys." He calmed down and immediately thereafter found the keys.

I was asleep when this took place, and Mike did not want to disturb me because I was recuperating from hip replacement surgery. Later that afternoon, while I was sitting out in the backyard reading a book, Mike called to tell me about his Kardinal Kraig encounter. I was so happy for him and could not help but think that it was just like Kraig to come up with so novel an approach to get his father's attention. While I was musing over that, with the open book still in my lap, an absolutely beautiful butterfly landed on the page in front of me! These little God touches are a constant reminder to us of Kraig's and God's love.

There have been so many beautiful expressions of love and concern from people near and far. A mother of one of Kraig's classmates made a stained-glass stepping stone depicting an angel holding a baseball bat. She brought it over to the house, and we placed it in the rose garden, the one we started the day Kraig made his First Communion. Trees, in memory of Kraig and two other students who have died, have been planted in the front of Mary Immaculate School. The area has been named *The Angel Garden*. The same mother who gave us the stained-glass angel made another one in school colors, which is placed in front of the tree planted for Kraig.

One tender memory Mike and I will forever cherish happened on the eve of Kraig's birthday, the first one we faced without him. The weather was lovely, and we decided to go over to the cemetery and spend some quiet time with Kraig.

We were not there very long when we saw Karl's friend, Matt, walking toward us with his father.

"What a surprise!" I said. "Here comes our home run champion."

When they got closer, I noticed that Matt was carrying something in his hand. As he approached the bench where we were sitting, he showed us the championship baseball he was awarded the night Kraig and I attended the game.

"I wanted Kraig to have this," he said.

His father sat down beside us and the three of us watched in silent admiration as Matt walked over and set the ball down next to Kraig's headstone. I could just hear Kraig letting out a big yelp: "This is so cool!" When Matt turned around, I walked over to hug him. Then Mike shook his hand and told him what a wonderful tribute it was to the special friendship he and Kraig had shared. Later, we put the baseball in a clear plastic display case to protect it from inclement weather.

Gratitude for the happiness that Kraig brought into the lives of all who really knew him is continually demonstrated in generous gestures like Matt's. Thoughtful remembrances, cards and letters, not to mention moose trinkets, continue to arrive at our door. It's a way for people to say, "We loved Kraig on earth and we still love him." Mike and I deeply appreciate every display of love that has been expressed and we continuously thank God for these blessings.

One final note ~ we wanted to have a small memorial to Kraig near the cabin in Colorado. A friend of ours handcrafted a beautiful wooden cross, which we erected on the mountain right above our bedroom. A brass plate on the cross reads:

Kraig James Frick
September 9,1987-September 17,1996
Our Little Prince   Our Little Saint

I found a small pair of brass moose antlers and had them attached to the cross. I knew that would please Kraig. He never once lost his childlike enthusiasm for anything connected with moose.

There is a passage from *The Little Prince*, the book I was reading to Kraig when he left this earth, which I hope and pray others will come to understand as we do. In the story, the Fox tells the Little Prince, "It is only with the heart that one can see rightly ~ what is essential is invisible to the eye."

From the moment I discovered that Kraig was ill, God lovingly led me every step of the way. Each and every prayer strengthened my faith, making it possible for me to recognize the gift of priesthood God wanted to bestow on Kraig in answer to Jacques' prayer. Why should such extravagance surprise us? Nothing is impossible with God. I remember reading how Padre Pio's constant companion was his Guardian Angel. No one saw the angel, yet, in faith, they believe he was there all the time. We do not see Kraig's physical presence, but we consider ourselves richly blessed to be able to see with our hearts that Kraig's spirit is alive and working side by side with Jacques in the "Moose Team." As a matter of fact, he is more alive than we are because eternal life perfects love.

Chapter XIII

He has made everything beautiful in its time.
(Eccles. 3:11)

Jacques remained in Japan for two and a half years as the assistant pastor at the Franciscan Chapel Center, a parish located in the Roppongi district of Tokyo. He was already familiar with this parish community, having served a nine-month internship there during his seminary training. While some of his parishioners were English-speaking Japanese, most were expatriates employed by major Japanese corporations, or young professionals teaching ESL (English as a Second Language). He could also count a number of housemaids and nannies, mostly from the Philippines, among the faithful. Filling the spiritual needs of such a diverse family would certainly pose a formidable challenge to any newly ordained priest. For Jacques, however, given his life experience and congenial nature, the assignment seemed tailor-made.

Still, nothing could have prepared him for the events that unfolded soon after his arrival.

A North American woman in great distress was

referred to the Franciscan Chapel Center for help and Jacques was the priest who counseled her. Over the course of their meetings, he discovered that the cause of her distress was a case of pedophilia. Her roommate, a man who was teaching in a Japanese private school for girls, had begun to manifest pedophile tendencies. Having suffered as an abused child herself, this knowledge tormented her to the point where she contemplated suicide.

It took a great deal of time and patience, but Jacques was finally able to persuade the woman to allow him to contact the school. The officials at the school were shocked by such an allegation and unwilling to believe that a highly respected teacher of theirs could have any connection with pedophilia. They agreed, however, to look into the matter. Their investigation brought to light a report that had been filed by another teacher at the school describing the man in question as photographing students in the gym, an activity that had apparently nothing to do with his job responsibilities.

For Jacques, this was only round one in a *David Facing Goliath* struggle. Through some contacts in the Diplomatic Corps, he discovered the existence of ECPAT (End Child Prostitution and Trafficking), an international organization that monitors child sexual abuse around the world. Jacques contacted representatives from ECPAT in Japan and then set up a meeting with the school officials. Despite the evidence they had uncovered, the school was informed that, without a victim, nothing could be done. This turned out to be a grave understatement. To his astonishment, Jacques learned that even with definite proof of pedophilia, there were no laws in Japan regarding child molestation. In fact, the age of consent in Tokyo was thirteen years old, and taking pictures of children to be used for pornography was not illegal!

The follow-up to this meeting carried Jacques deeper into the tragic reality of the child pornography market. From ECPAT Headquarters in Bangkok, he learned that child pornography was a billion dollar industry in Japan with businessmen making a fortune on the backs of children. Further information from Interpol (International Police Force) revealed that a staggering 80% of all child pornography in the world was produced in Japan.

Something had to be done, but where to start? For nearly ten years, the Japanese themselves had attempted, without success to ban child pornography. As Jacques pursued the matter, he was amazed to find roadblocks and resistance from among his own peers. People were reluctant to get involved in a dossier on pornographic activity that was larger than any single individual or parish. Yet despite the reticence of some, there were many, within and outside of the parish who desperately wanted to eradicate this blight from Japan.

The enormity of the problem and the scarcity of help available weighed heavily on Jacques. He agonized over his participation in this battle. In prayer, he gave everything into the hands of God, knowing that only heaven had the power and the means to conquer such an evil. But what did God expect of him? What, if anything, did God want him to do? Walk away and leave it alone, or throw himself in up to the neck?

The answer came ~ clear and resonant ~ in a manner that Jacques could neither overlook nor misinterpret. One day at Mass, as he knelt among the congregation, Jacques was again begging God for guidance. In his turmoil, his eyes filled with tears and his head sunk into his hands. At that moment, the celebrant raised the chalice to consume the Precious Blood of Jesus. Jacques glanced up and was startled by the sight of Kraig's face. Unbeknownst to Jacques, the priest celebrating Mass had taken his chalice from the sacristy. Spiritual energy filled Jacques' whole being. He knew what he had to do. He also knew that he would not be facing Goliath alone. In his heart, he heard Kraig promise:

"Remember, I will help you. I am part of your ministry, and together we will conquer this."

Nothing had happened by accident. Jacques' presence in Japan and the special ministry that he shared with Kraig was all part of the Divine plan. Jacques remembered Kraig's little prayer asking

God to help those most in need. Who could be more in need than a little, defenseless child in the hands of such ruthless profiteering? Kraig's prayer took on special significance for the fight to save the victims of sexual abuse. Jacques knew that he was called by God to this work, and that Kraig was going to be his biggest ally.

Jacques' gifts for organization came into play immediately. He took the offensive position and determined to fight on all fronts. A trip to the Canadian Embassy revealed that the accused teacher had a record for having made pornographic films using his own children! The Embassy was willing to hand the file over to the Japanese police, but the police continued to maintain that they could do nothing as long as the law saw no crime in the man's activities. Jacques moved the battle to the next level. The school devised a new employment policy requiring all teachers to supply a security profile from their respective embassies. Everyone except the suspect complied with the request. The school was now free to terminate the man's contract.

So far, so good. One child abuser was out of service, but what about the national "open season on children" that was going on all the time? Jacques knew he had to go all the way to the top. He initiated a vigorous campaign among Japan's highest and mightiest. He met with Prime Minister Obuchi in a private interview and expressed his concern about the lack of protection for children in Japan and the exploitation within Japan of children from other countries. It was a most gratifying meeting. Jacques also drummed up the support of Japanese officials and their families, members of the Diplomatic Corps in Tokyo, ambassadors and their wives from countries around the world, churches of various faiths, and organizations like *Doctors without Borders*. Enormous international pressure was exerted on Japan.

Nor did Jacques forget the immediate needs of children already or about to be swallowed up by the body snatchers on Japan's streets. The parishioners from the Franciscan Chapel Center helped him put together a Street Children Ministry that eventually received worldwide recognition through ECPAT headquarters. Jacques advocated attacking the root of the problem and rescuing children before victimization took place. To that end, funds were raised to help children from poor countries who were being exploited, giving them an alternative to the prostitution offered by members of the Japanese Mafia.

Jacques put technology to work, too, and thanks to the Internet, not only Japanese children but children from all over the world could be rescued. The story about Jacques' effort against child pornography was picked up in the international press. His name and picture appeared in newspapers and TV newscasts all over Asia,

Europe, North and South America and Africa!

After eight months of intense labor, just in time for Easter, what had seemed absolutely impossible at the outset was finally accomplished. The Japanese Diet passed a law making child pornography illegal in Japan. Already, this law has succeeded in closing down many of the studios and websites that produced such material. At the Franciscan Chapel Center, they call it their "Easter Miracle."

Jacques doesn't mind telling people that the success of this campaign is owed, not to the personal initiative of any one person, or the intervention of the rich, famous and powerful, but to a little boy named Kraig, whose prayers before God worked miracles for the children of Japan and the world.

God has a delightful sense of humor. During the height of the battle, when press releases were front-page items in all the Japanese newspapers, Jacques would clip the articles and mail them to Mike and me. In many of these articles, Kraig's name was mentioned as the inspiration behind the battle. One day, while I was making a copy of one of these articles, I happened to glance down at its reverse side as it lay on the copy machine. Staring right back up at me was a photo of a moose chasing a police cruiser in Bennington, Vermont! I made no attempt to suppress my excitement and let out a shout right there in the store. When I got home, I immediately telephoned Mike to tell him that our little angel, Kraig, had sent us a message. Jacques let me know later that there are no moose in Japan and, as far as he could recall, he never once heard a Japanese person talk about moose. For him, finding this picture was a personal little "pat on the back" from Kraig to let him know that he was truly working behind the scenes.

Getting a law passed, against all odds, in a foreign country would probably rank as the most dramatic manifestation of Kraig's help, but it was certainly not the only incident where Jacques relied on Kraig to bring aid where it was most needed.

Jacques met Francois and Gael Leger through their son, a student in the Franciscan Chapel religion class, and they became fast friends. Francois was assigned to the French Embassy in Tokyo, and at the time Jacques met them, Gail was expecting. The family went back to France for the birth of not one but three babies! Upon their return to Tokyo, however, the Leger triplets became very ill. The diagnosis was meningitis and the prognosis was grim. Jacques included the triplets in the prayers for the faithful at every Mass, and he asked the children of the parish to pray as hard as they could. Word spread rapidly and an outpouring of prayer emanated from churches all over Tokyo. Mike and 1 also added our own and the prayers of others in the United States. In particular, I enlisted the aid of the school children at Mary Immaculate.

Sadly, however, there was no improvement. The day finally came when Francois telephoned Jacques and asked him to come administer the Last Rites of the Church to his three children.

Before leaving for the Leger home, Jacques went into the chapel to pray. As always, he turned to his partner Kraig for help. What could they do for the Leger triplets? Thoughts of Blessed Marie of the Incarnation popped into his mind. Her special charism had been her devotion and love for children. She taught many of the young girls and Indian children of the colony of New France at the beginning of the history of Canada. With this in mind, Jacques asked Kraig:

"Go . . . visit Blessed Marie of the Incarnation and tell her that we desperately need her intercession. Remind her that, as one of the Blessed, she has special powers in heaven. Please, Kraig, plead my case with her!"

Jacques' heart swelled with peace. He had complete confidence that Kraig, whom he knew personally, and Blessed Marie, whom he held in such high esteem, could intercede to the Sacred Heart of Jesus and the Immaculate Heart of Mary and ask for a miracle in a way far more powerful than he could. He got up off his knees and walked out to meet Francois, who had come to the chapel to pick him up. They went first to the family's home to bless Capucine and Emma, two of the three babies. Little Louis, the boy, was still in an incubator at the hospital. Jacques anointed the two infants and, together with Francois and Gael, prayed over each child. When he had finished, the three of them left for the hospital.

As Jacques looked down at Louis, he couldn't help but observe that his tiny chest was barely moving. In fact, there were moments when it seemed as if he had stopped breathing altogether. Jacques, Francois and Gael joined hands forming a circle around the incubator. With so much at stake, the intensity of emotion had reached fever pitch. A prayer of hope and trust poured forth from Jacques' heart. Reaching into the pocket of his habit, he scooped up Kraig's rosary into his hands. He wanted to touch Louis with the beads as he had done with Capucine and Emma. He later said that the presence of Kraig's spirit at that moment was stronger than he had ever experienced while in Japan. As he touched the baby, there was no doubt in his mind that his priest partner was there beside him. Once again, he implored Kraig to make supplication in heaven to spare all three children.

Today, the Leger triplets are healthy and thriving.

Jacques is convinced that the combined prayers of all, sparked by a child named Kraig, were catapulted to heaven. The family is eternally grateful to all those, known and unknown, who formed this prayer crusade. Mike and I received a personal note of thanks from the Legers, along with a picture of the triplets. I went to Kraig's school to personally thank his classmates who had joined in the vigil of prayer for the babies. I marveled at the invisible links of prayer that had united children a world apart.

Jacques spent only two and a half years in Japan before returning to the United States, but in that short time he certainly made his mark.

Before departing Japan, Jacques was guest of honor for a "Sayonara" celebration. A former parish council president told him that he had never seen so many children attend a "Sayonara." Jacques smiled graciously and then, looking around the room at so many happy little faces, he suddenly found himself thinking about the theme of Kraig's resurrection Mass, "Let the Children Come Unto Me..." He remembered the vivid image he had experienced before the funeral, of children flocking to Kraig, who was sitting on the lap of Jesus. It was almost as if the image was coming to life before his eyes. Kraig had been with Jacques every step of the way in Japan. On the altar every day, through the grace of their common chalice, and in all the moments of petition and praise that had marked the dramatic events of the last two years, they were the "Moose Team." When celebrating Mass at the Franciscan Chapel Center, Jacques would often invite the children around the altar. In his instruction on the Eucharist, he used Kraig's chalice and shared Kraig's story with the children.

Many parents had confided to Jacques how their children would awaken them early on Sunday mornings, so anxious were they to attend Mass.

In July of 1999, Jacques returned to the United States, and spent a few days with us at our cabin in Colorado. It was a poignant reunion of friendship and prayer. Jacques celebrated Mass in the very room where he had first met Kraig. Mike and I brought him to the spot on the mountain where we had gone to pray after that first wonderful day when we had met him. Jacques, in turn, took us back to St. Malo's, to the area in the woods by a waterfall where he, too, had gone to pray after that providential meeting. These places have become sacred to all of us.

One night, shortly before leaving Colorado, Jacques was suddenly awakened. Unable to get back to sleep, he picked up his journal and wrote the following entry:

July 16, 1999, 2:30A.M.

"While celebrating Mass with the Frick family in the room where I first met Kraig, it became evident to all of us that as we continue to praise the greater glory of God through Kraig's chalice so, too, will we continue to lift up forever within our hearts stories of Moose and Miracles."

Chapter XIV

A Time to Dance (Eccles. 3:4)

Before embarking on his new assignment, Jacques set out for the family cottage in Northern Maine, not far from the Canadian border. The cottage is situated in the moose-populated woods overlooking the beautiful and wild shores of Long Lake, where loons, eagles, ducks and peace seekers, like himself, share a natural sanctuary. He needed some quiet time and rest before accepting a new assignment. His successful campaign in Tokyo to fight child pornography and prostitution, a campaign that culminated in Japan's first *ever* national legislation against such criminal practices, left him exhausted. It was May, the month that is officially regarded as spring in Northern Maine and Canada. However, there was no feeling of *springtime* in Jacques' heart. It felt more like he was carrying the weight of an arduous Canadian winter on his shoulders. He had never expected being a priest would have pitted him against a billion dollar industry involving thousands of innocent children, not only in Japan, but from around the world. The emotional baggage from the Tokyo experience still haunted him, leaving him lonely, unsettled, and seriously lacking any sense of purpose and direction. What next? Where next? These questions kept spinning in his brain, robbing him of all peace.

This was precisely the state of mind he was in when he decided one morning to go for a long, solitary walk on the wooded, gravel road in the back of the cottage. After an hour had passed, he came to a deserted beach, where Long Lake ends in Van Buren Cove. Continuing to walk along the shore until he reached the mouth of Mud Brook, he stopped and stood still. At Mud Brook, the walking path ends and an extensive marsh begins. The marsh is home to numerous and varied species of birds. He spotted an old dry log and quickly sat down to rest his tired feet. The birds immediately began to chirp their disapproval over this sudden intrusion during their crucial mating season. The resounding anxieties of the birds soon echoed in Jacques' restless heart. It was impossible to remain still in the midst of such a heavy barrage of diving wings and piercing shrieks. He briskly bolted from the log and headed back to the lake shore, along the same path that he had just walked a few minutes earlier. *Something was different,* he thought! Approaching the water's edge, he noticed enormous patches of yellow spreading like a blanket on the graveled sand. The scene piqued his curiosity and he crept closer to investigate. Suddenly, the patches of vivid color came alive. He stood in awe as hundreds of beautiful black and yellow monarch butterflies took flight, forming a domino-like effect all along the shore line. In a matter of seconds, he found himself surrounded by a multitude of butterflies. Like a flash, Jacques' mind, heart and soul became submerged in pure Franciscan joy. At that moment, in a graced mystical way, he felt his priesthood united in perfect harmony with Kraig's heavenly priesthood. It was as if a wave had washed over him and he knew it was the Holy Spirit! The feeling rushed from his heart to his lips in prayer:

As instruments of Your most holy compassion, we your humble Franciscan servants at the Chapel Center, thank you Lord for all the precious souls of so many innocent children who, through our prayers and petitions to You, our loving Lord, will be spared sexual abuse and exploitation.

Through this profound enlightenment, Jacques understood that the magnificent butterflies, a symbol of Christ's Resurrection, were a sign of God's hope and love for each of his children; these same children for whom (with Kraig and Blessed Marie of the Incarnation's constant spiritual presence and assistance) he had prayed so diligently and worked so persistently during his assignment at the Chapel Center in Tokyo. Through his shared priesthood with Kraig, God had chosen to confirm that wherever he goes, whatever he does, if he looks and listens closely enough, God will be there at his side. TRUSTING in God always sets one free!

Chapter XV

A Time To Speak (Eccles. 3:7)

[Author's Reflections]

It has been five years since *Of Moose and Miracles* was first published. During that time, I have kept in close touch with the Fricks as well as Fr. Jacques.

Three of Karyl and Mike's children, Ginger, Bri and Klaire, have gotten married, with Jacques presiding over each of their weddings. Three additional grandchildren have been born and, with another on the way, the Frick clan will soon number 18! Mike Frick is now retired and this frees Karyl and Mike up for more traveling, most of which involves visiting one or another of their children. They are also heavily committed to helping out the Missionaries of Charity. On a recent visit to Dallas, Fr. Jacques stayed with the Fricks and had the privilege of celebrating Mass at the Missionaries of Charity Chapel. Having already been familiar with *Of Moose and Miracles*, it was a special blessing for the

Missionary Sisters to meet Jacques and participate in a Mass where he used the paten and chalice bearing Kraig's name and picture. There are still gatherings at the Frick household and, on special occasions, the family meets at their cabin, the *Quiet Moose*, in the beautiful mountains of Colorado. These get-togethers provide a lot of support for Karyl, Mike and the entire Frick clan.

After the book was published, Father Jacques lost his father, Fernand, from a heart attack. As much as this saddened him, he will forever be grateful for the miraculous healing from cancer his father had experienced. It was an event that not only fortified his faith but cemented his bond with the Frick family.

Many people have taken the time to thank us (Karyl, Jacques and myself) for the book. One man, from California, called Karyl to tell her personally how touched he was with Kraig's story. Just recently, a man from Maine called me to say how much the book had meant to him. And there have been so many beautiful letters from readers who took the time to express their feelings. Perhaps the most gratifying response was one experienced by both Jacques and me from two separate sources. While stationed in Tokyo, a woman approached Jacques to tell him that she had abandoned the idea of having an abortion after reading the book. Back here in the States, a close friend of mine called me long-distance to report that she had given the book to an acquaintance who, in turn, had passed it on to a troubled young woman. This young woman was scheduled to have an abortion but she changed her mind after finishing the book. These are blessings beyond price and we thank God for them.

Moose, stuffed and otherwise, have taken on a whole new meaning to those of us personally involved with the story and, I might add, to readers all over the country. I remember while writing the book, the title popped into my head one day. Obviously a play on the words [*Of Mice and Men*] by the famous author, John Steinbeck, they nevertheless just seemed to fit. I discussed my idea with Karyl, worried that perhaps such a title might not be dignified enough. Karyl has always been enchanted with Kraig's love affair with his little moose family and she gave me her blessing immediately. Looking back, I have to believe the title was inspired. Whenever I run into a picture, a statue, or a little stuffed moose, I am reminded of Kraig's presence in my life. Many readers have shared similar feelings with me. As for the Frick family, they still experience "moose bumps" every time they encounter one of these creatures.

It happened to Klaire while honeymooning in Hawaii. She was out running early one morning. It was the last day of her honeymoon and she was distracted by a sense of sadness that kept intruding into her thoughts. This was truly the happiest time in her life, yet she found herself fighting back tears. Memories of Kraig were swirling in her mind and she found it hard to accept the fact that he had not been present to share in her joy. Reprimanding herself, she shook her head, refusing to give into such doleful feelings. At just that moment, she looked straight ahead and noticed a man running toward her, dressed like a moose! In Hawaii? Baffled, Klaire stopped in her tracks. The man was handing out flyers for a new restaurant called, "Moose McGillicuttys." She enthusiastically accepted a flyer, then immediately headed to the restaurant and ordered take-out breakfasts for herself and her husband. On her way back to the hotel, she gazed up at the sky and broke into laughter. Klaire knew that somehow Kraig had managed this *coincidence* from above just to let her know that he **was** sharing in the joy of this important time of her life. I truly believe our loved ones, who are safely nestled in the arms of God, are closer to us than we can imagine.

Jacques also shared a wonderful moose story with me. It was about a year after his "butterfly" experience and, once again, he was visiting his family cottage in Maine. Driving in the deep woods surrounding Long Lake, on his way to Saint-Leonard, he actually came face-to-face with a bull moose standing on the dirt road. The moose was munching on tall grass in a small pool of water beside the narrow road. Leaving all precaution aside, Fr. Jacques slowly moved his 4 X 4 vehicle forward until he came right up next to the moose. It didn't budge an inch, but kept feeding on the grass. As if it were a perfectly natural thing to do, Jacques lowered the window on the driver's side. With a mere stretch of his hand, he could easily have touched this enormous animal. He turned off the engine and continued to watch while the moose tranquilly grazed away. Suddenly, the moose realized he was not alone. Raising its head, the moose turned to face Jacques and stared at him intently. "I had absolutely no fear," Jacques told me. "As a matter of fact, I felt an incredible sense of peace and I stared right back at this huge behemoth now facing me. The words from Scripture, *And the lion shall lie down with the lamb...* poured into my heart and I thanked God for the grace of the moment. I was certain that Kraig, my little mystical companion, was aware of the scene taking place. What a gift to be able to share in Kraig's joy and humor! My Franciscan habit was draped on the back seat and I knew that Kraig's rosary (the one Karyl had given to me the night before the funeral) was tucked inside the breast pocket. I reached back and grabbed hold of the beads. As if inspired, I prayed from the deepest part of my heart for God's little children around the world. I remained in awe and prayer for at least 15 minutes. Then, quietly and without fanfare, 'Kraig Moose' re-entered the woods and I, son of St. Francis (patron saint of animals) continued on my journey to Saint-Leonard."

Father Jacques' shared vocation with Kraig has taken him to many places. Upon his return from Japan, he was eventually sent to New York City where he ministered to Haitian families. During that period, through continued support of the Street Children Committee in Tokyo and Project Oasis in Dallas, many at-risk children received donations for housing, food, medical assistance, school supplies and thousands of [mostly new] books in over twenty countries around the world.

On to a new assignment in Silver Spring, Maryland, Jacques founded the African and Haitian Catholic community of Marie-Reine-du-Monde. With Kraig's spirit always at his side, he set up the first free health clinic for French speaking immigrant families in the greater Washington, D.C. and Baltimore areas. He also established a free immigration outreach center and scholarships for African children at St. Camillus Catholic School in Silver Spring, Md. Donations from the Kraig Frick Memorial Fund have helped to support these various projects.

As a board member of MCAP (Maryland Coalition Against Pornography), Jacques lobbied with the Archdiocese of Washington, D.C. and the Maryland District Attorney's office for tougher laws against pornography. He was also instrumental in bringing into focus a serious problem of prostitution of young people in a poor, mostly Catholic neighborhood. A Catholic Youth and Family Outreach Center has since been opened in that particular neighborhood. Jacques continues to pray daily for the welfare of abused or at-risk children around the world. He also continues to have faith in the strong intercessory powers of Kraig and his team of little angels in heaven, along with Blessed Mother Marie of the Incarnation, his Ursuline spiritual mother. Together, they form a mighty prayer league!

From Maryland, Jacques returned to his home town of Saint-Leonard located on the Maine-New Brunswick border. Once again, working with refugees, he promoted immigration in rural communities. One successful endeavor was with the Rutayisire family, originally from Rwanda (parents of 5 boys), who successfully established a home and business in St. Leonard. In 2006, Jacques left the responsibility of this organization to a local lay board. His true ministry at this time in his life was to serve as a Spiritual Director at the Christian Life Center in Frenchville, Maine. It is there where he and Kraig succeeded in spreading the Good News of Christ through the Cursillo movement, retreats, spiritual direction, prayer services, the sacrament of reconciliation and the Eucharist. Many people from the St. John Valley, throughout Maine and parts of New Brunswick, received various spiritual healings from the "Moose Team Mission" of Kraig and Jacques at the Christian Life Center. *Of Moose and Miracles* soon became a favorite source of spiritual reading for many families and Kraig became well known as a favorite intercessor for many prayer intentions.

Presently, Jacques and Kraig are very busy setting up a new pastoral outreach center for French families living in the greater New York City metro area. Kraig continues to send "hints from heaven" at just the moment Jacques needs reassurance. Initiating a new outreach center in an area the size of New York City is a daunting task. Feeling somewhat homesick and a little insecure, Jacques was out walking one morning when he came upon a store. He saw a sign with a big bird engraved on it--a cardinal of course! What a cardinal has to do with kitchen renovations and cabinet making he wasn't quite sure...but it did give him a hearty laugh. Kraig was letting him know, just as he had in times past, that he was right there with him. Jacques' feelings of insecurity were immediately replaced with hope and enthusiasm for this newest challenge.

There have been many instances when Karyl, Mike and their children have felt Kraig's presence. It never ceases to amaze them how Kraig has used what Jacques has dubbed his *Franciscan charism with animals* to send little messages here on earth-- butterflies, cardinals, moose--they all serve one purpose--to give them hope!

Of Moose and Miracles

The story of Jacques' and Kraig's priesthood continues to move on, always for the greater glory of God's name.

Marion Lee

To order additional copies of this book:
Please complete the form below and send to:

CMJ Marian Publishers & Distributors
P.O. Box 661 • Oak Lawn, IL 60454
Toll free 888-636-6799
Call 708-636-2995 or fax 708-636-2855
Email: jwby@aol.com
www.cmjbooks.com

Name:_____

Address:_____

City:_____

Phone:(   ) _____

Of Moose and Miracles